VICTORIA ILLUSTRATED

VICTORIA ILLUSTRATED
1857 & 1862

Engravings from the original editions by S.T. GILL & N. CHEVALIER

Introduction and notes by W.H. Newnham

Lansdowne Press

First published 1971 by
LANSDOWNE PRESS PTY LTD
346 St Kilda Road Melbourne 3004
© Lansdowne Press Pty Ltd
Type set in Bembo by
Dudley E. King Melbourne
Printed and bound in Hong Kong
Designed by Derrick I. Stone

SBN 7018 0300 2

THE BOOKS AND THE ENGRAVINGS

The first volume of *Victoria Illustrated* carries the imprint: 'Published by Sands & Kenny, Melbourne & Sydney, Thomas Brown, Geelong, 1857'. Presumably the success of the album led to the publication in 1862 of the second volume, which was titled *Victoria Illustrated: Second Series*. The first volume consisted exclusively of engravings but in the second series there is a descriptive text for each plate.

In the present edition the two volumes have been combined; a few engravings have been deleted to avoid duplication of subject matter. Part One contains the engravings from the first series of *Victoria Illustrated* and those from the second series make up the second part. In the second series the original commentary is printed in roman face in the left-hand column. The headings follow the style, spelling and punctuation of the original volumes.

Neither Gill nor Chevalier did the engraving. They drew the scenes and their sketches were copied on to the steel or copper plates by the engravers, A. Willmore and J. Tingle. The original plates have been lost long ago. In this edition the engravings have been reproduced by photo-lithography, a process which gives the most satisfactory rendering of the originals, and fractionally enlarged to improve definition. Copies of the original editions were kindly made available by the Latrobe Library, Melbourne.

VICTORIA ILLUSTRATED

Entrance to Port Phillip.

PUBLISHED BY SANDS & KENNY, MELBOURNE & SYDNEY,

THOMAS BROWN, GEELONG.

1857.

THE GOLDEN YEARS & S. T. GILL

They were golden years in Victoria, the ten years which began in 1851—years brought to life by these engravings published in 1857 and 1862 in elegant editions of Victoria Illustrated. In ten fabulous and exciting years, gold transformed this quiet pastoral district into a world-famous Eldorado. In the first full year of production (1852) more than 4,000,000 ounces of gold worth £20,000,000 (or about $80,000,000 today) were accounted for, and for the next ten years Victoria produced a third of the world's gold.

In the gold rush from Britain, Europe, America and Asia to Victoria there came all kinds and classes of men; adventurers, tradesmen, shopkeepers, labourers, the well-to-do, the middle-class and the poor, politicians of the old order and rebels of a new one. And of course, artists. Two of them were the men whose work illustrates this book—Samuel Thomas Gill, a Somerset man, and Nicholas Chevalier who was born in Russia although his father was a Swiss. In Gill's work we see primarily the men and women of the gold rush days and the life they found and made here; much of Chevalier's work shows how the wealth from gold transformed the local architectural scene.

The discovery of gold in Victoria was officially announced on 5 July 1851. By October, Melbourne and Geelong and their large suburbs seemed nearly emptied of men. Not only the idlers and day labourers threw up their jobs and ran off to the diggings; so did responsible tradesmen, farmers, clerks and 'not a few of the superior classes', to quote Governor La Trobe's report to London. 'Cottages are deserted, houses to let, and business is at a standstill and even schools are closed. In some of the suburbs not a man is left and women, for their own protection, group together to keep house. The ships in the harbour are in great measure deserted.'

Police and prison warders joined in the madness. By the end of the year, despite tempting increases of salary, only eleven Melbourne policemen remained on duty. Labourers were being offered £4 a day; a man would have felt wealthy with such pay. The Governor and the Bishop of Melbourne had to groom their own horses.

Prices soared like the miners' hopes. Hay rose twenty-fold; butter became nearly ten times dearer. At times it cost up to £100 a ton to send a drayload from Melbourne to Bendigo, 100 miles away. Many farmers complained that it was more expensive to send their produce to Melbourne than to have it shipped from Liverpool. Other farmers, close to the goldfields, made a fortune by selling locally.

Four days before the discovery of gold was officially announced, the Port Phillip District became the independent colony of Victoria; previously it had been part of the mother colony of New South Wales. The battle for separation had been long and bitter and many contended that the official 'discovery' of gold had been withheld deliberately until separation had been granted.

With the finding of gold, Victoria's population rose dramatically from 77,000 to 540,000 in ten years—an increase that was not to be equalled in Victoria for one hundred years. By 1861, almost half of Australia's population was in Victoria, and Melbourne had become Australia's biggest city. Its population had jumped from 23,000 to 130,000.

In 1851, the only large town outside Melbourne was Geelong with a population of 8,000. Portland had about 1,000, Port Fairy about 950 and Warrnambool 350, while the whole of Gippsland had only 2,000. Inland towns like Bacchus Marsh, Hamilton, Kilmore, Kyneton, Colac, Sale and Benalla had small populations but the remainder was thinly spread across a thousand or more unfenced sheep and cattle runs. Ten years later, Geelong had forged ahead to 23,000 while great gold towns like Ballarat (22,000), Bendigo (13,000) and Castlemaine (11,000) had settled down to a more permanent existence. So too had the smaller gold centres of Creswick, Inglewood, Maryborough, Ararat and Maldon. The seaports of Portland, Port Fairy and Warrnambool had developed, and a few farming townships had edged up past the 1,000 population mark. Even so, forty-two per cent of the population still lived in gold towns or on the diggings.

In Melbourne men out to rake in money were only too pleased to provide means of satisfying the luckier miners who wished to eat or drink at any hour of the day or night in the company of ladies delighted to help them to spend their money as spectacularly, and almost as quickly, as it had been found. Gaudy shops, bands and musicians of a dozen countries, theatres and amusement gardens, the sound of building everywhere and the rush of traffic emphasised the bursting vitality of a capital city.

In 1854 the first Australian railway—only three miles long—was opened in Melbourne by the new Governor, Sir Charles Hotham. Telegraphic communications were introduced, the University of Melbourne and the Melbourne Public Library were founded on 3 July, and measures introduced to offset a trade depression appeared to be effective. Imports were more firmly controlled than in 1853, when they exceeded exports by £5,000,000.

The extraordinary prosperity attracted many criminals. 'The roads swarm with bushrangers and crimes of the most fearful kind abound', complained the Argus. 'In broad daylight men are knocked down and robbed.' In one issue twelve columns were devoted to details of stolen horses.

On the goldfields, the miners were on the point of open revolt. They were angry about having to pay for a mining licence without having the right to vote, and about police brutality in checking licence holders. Faults on both sides precipitated the tragic Eureka Stockade fight at Ballarat in 1854, where troops swiftly crushed the miners' rebellion. Five soldiers and about thirty miners died. But the miners won a moral victory and later many of their demands were met.

By 1856, when the next Governor, Sir Henry Barkly, arrived, Victoria was not only more prosperous, but more peaceful. The first Parliament House chambers had been completed, new bridges added across the Yarra, water reticulated and imposing public buildings completed. The first public schools, Scotch College, Melbourne Grammar School and Geelong Grammar School, were already established and Scotch and Melbourne Grammar had in 1858 played what was to become the first game of Australian Rules football. By 1861, trains were taking racegoers to Flemington to see the first Melbourne Cup.

Until 1858, the chief item of governmental expenditure was main road construction. With the better roads came improved transport and the era of Cobb and Co. coaches with their superb drivers and teams of thoroughbred horses that won a deserved reputation for speed and punctuality.

The city had improved its amenities, and hotels like the Grand Imperial, made famous by the notorious dancer and actress Lola Montez, and the Royal, were in world class. By 1853, the Royal had become the home of Americans who had invaded Melbourne during the gold rushes. Samuel Moss renamed the Royal the Criterion and introduced American bartenders who mixed exciting new cocktails with exotic names, and persuaded world visitors that their 'southern' drinks, such as mint juleps, could not be bettered in Paris, Vienna, New York or London.

The Criterion had a vast and lofty Grecian billiard room, a bowling alley, marble counters and monster claret cups, as well as a special bridal suite at £100 a week. On the Glorious Fourth in July 1854, the American community celebrating national independence had set Melbourne by the ears—and this took some doing then—by sitting down to breakfast in full evening dress and continuing to eat, drink and make speeches till dawn the following day.

Music and theatre were well patronised. The chorus of the Melbourne Philharmonic Society was praised by overseas musicians. George Coppin, entrepreneur and actor, brought out a grand opera company in 1855 which presented a variety of productions from Lucia di Lammermoor to The Bohemian Girl. In the same year, Coppin arranged for a fine English actor G. V. Brooke to play Shakespearean roles for the sum of £10,000 for 100 performances. Meanwhile a clever colonial actor, G. H. Rogers, was packing the 3,000 seats of The Royal with polished performances in School for Scandal. The years 1855 to 1860 probably saw some of the finest theatre ever presented in Victoria.

Churches were well attended. The gold rushes brought no decline in congregations. By 1861, a quarter of the population was regularly attending church—twice as many as before gold was found. Church parades in many of the gold centres and townships became a feature of country life. The area under cultivation had risen impressively from 57,000 acres in 1851 to 440,000 acres ten years later when the holders numbered 13,000 against the earlier 3,000.

All this would seem to suggest unrelieved general progress and prosperity, but in 1857, unemployment among unskilled migrants plagued the colony. Union leaders fought strenuously against any reduction in wages. By 1857, more than twenty unions were active.

Much has been written of the progressive democratic and social movements in Victoria at this time—the gaining of the eight-hour working day, the improvement of working conditions, the acceptance of the secret ballot, adult voting franchise, establishment of free, secular and compulsory education, the rights of workers, and the formation of unions. But Victoria had no monopoly of such movements. A number of countries had adopted similar measures.

As in other Australian colonies, more than ninety per cent of migrants were British. An important difference in Victoria was the high proportion of well-educated and skilled artisans. In 1861, only 11 per cent of the Colony's population was illiterate, lower than in London or in any other British Colony, and less than half the average in the United Kingdom. Many migrants were attracted not only by the lure of gold but by the hope of better working conditions. Influenced by Chartism, they brought with them a determination for equality which cut across the prejudices of an established gentry.

The toughness and recklessness of the Australian miner have often been exaggerated; Lord Robert Cecil, later Earl of Salisbury and three times Prime Minister of Britain, wrote when touring the goldfields that 'I found less crime than in a large English town and more order and civility than I have witnessed in my own native village, Hatfield'. Nor were the Chinese (and there were more than 42,000 of them in Victoria at one time, representing eight per cent of the population) poorly educated coolies. Rather, they were farmers, small traders, peasants and mechanics who borrowed money, submitted themselves to organised supervision and gave a lien on their services or labour until their debt was cleared.

But the miners, of course were not Victoria's first migrants. The first settlers in the Port Phillip District had come seeking not gold but land for grazing sheep and cattle.

In 1827, a well known Tasmanian settler, John Batman, had written without success to the Governor of New South Wales asking for a grant of Victorian land in exchange for promises of stocking by sheep and cattle. Eight years later, a syndicate of fifteen men calling itself the Port Phillip Association, and headed by John Batman, took the law into its own hands and decided to squat on the rich grazing lands of southern Victoria.

Although the Henty Brothers from Tasmania had founded a permanent settlement at Portland in 1834, the beginning of Victoria dates from 7 June 1835, when Batman and his party, having sailed from Launceston, Tasmania, negotiated with the chiefs of several tribes near the Merri Creek, about five miles from Melbourne, for the purchase of some 600,000 acres of good grazing land. Carefully-prepared documents were marked with crosses to confirm this transfer for approximately £200 worth of knives, tomahawks, blankets, mirrors, scissors, red shirts, flannel jackets and flour. Although Batman always insisted that Aborigines from Sydney who were with him explained the conditions to the local people, it is very doubtful whether they understood.

The following day, 8 June, was spent exploring the Yarra River. Writing of that day, Batman put down in his diary his modest prophecy, 'this will be the place for a village'. However, no one knows whether he went with the boat crew up the river. When Batman returned to Tasmania he did not leave his party on the future site of Melbourne, but at Indented Head, some forty miles away, near Geelong. A month later John Pascoe Fawkner, the rival claimant to the title of founder of Melbourne, set out from Tasmania with adequate supplies and provisions to found a settlement, but had to be put ashore because he became violently seasick in bad weather. His party continued on in the Enterprise and by 29 August 1835 they had found the Yarra and were unloading the stores—which included three and a half gallons of gin—near the site where the Customs House was later built in Flinders Street. Thus, at Melbourne's founding, neither famous pioneer was present. Fawkner arrived to settle on 11 October and Batman followed four weeks later, on 6 November.

The first settlers had already been warned that they were 'trespassers, liable to be dealt with in like manner as other intruders upon the vacant lands of the Crown in the said colony'. The 'said colony' was New South Wales; its Governor, Sir Richard Bourke, lived in the capital, Sydney. The settlers ignored the warnings.

S.T.Gill, delt.

J.Tingle sc.

Ballaarat Flat, from the Black Hill.

Published by Sands & Kenny, Melbourne & Sydney, 1857.

Batman, who died three years after the foundation of Melbourne, is far better known than Fawkner who became the father of Melbourne and lived on for thirty years. Perhaps the reason for the legends that surround Batman is simply that he was a handsome, courageous and likeable man, sociable and convivial—the sort of man Australians still admire. Fawkner, on the other hand, was small, thin-lipped, bigoted, garrulous, a determined fighter, respected but little loved. Batman died on 6 May 1839, embittered and angry that he should have ended his life as an invalid . . . 'his last few months drawn to church in an invalid's chair on wheels . . . always till then jolly and sociable . . . a man who could never shun the festive board'.

Batman's disappointments began when the New South Wales government refused to recognise his claim to the land he had bought from the Aborigines. However, Governor Bourke, saw that he could do nothing to halt the inflow of settlers and recognised the existence of the township which by June, 1836, had a population of 177. Its inhabitants owned 26,500 sheep and livestock worth £80,000—an average holding of £2,400, a considerable sum in those days. The first magistrate, Captain William Lonsdale, arrived in October 1836, when, in a second census, Constable James Dwyer counted the population of 224, comprising 210 Protestants, fourteen Roman Catholics and 'no pagans'. The first overlanders from the district of New South Wales also arrived at the end of 1836, crossing the Yarra at what is now Dight's Falls at Collingwood.

The most exciting event of the earliest years was the arrival in 1837 from Sydney of Sir Richard Bourke, who named the township Melbourne, after Queen Victoria's Prime Minister, and authorised the first sales of land on 1 June 1837. The average price of the first 100 half-acre allotments was £35. Seven blocks of Williamstown land sold on the same day averaged £46, indicating the hopes that this seaport, named after Britain's reigning monarch William IV, would become the capital—a hope blighted because the area lacked fresh water.

By 1839, the first of several land booms brought with it golden-tongued auctioneers. 'Be blindfolded, then when the hands are removed, you will conceive yourself translated into an enchanted land', one declared. 'Melbourne is always full of lovely colours and flowers because winter's chill is never felt and the ardent rays of the sun are cooled by the placid zephyrs rising from the beauteous banks of the Yarra', said another.

In October, 1839, Charles Joseph La Trobe arrived as Superintendent of the Port Phillip District. His appointment by London at the request of Governor Bourke was a recognition of the growing importance of the settlement. La Trobe was, in effect, a Lieutenant Governor, although he was not given this title until 1850. After speeches of welcome on a wretchedly cold and wet day, the sun came out. The town took on a festive air, added to by an Aboriginal corroboree near the site of St Francis' Church.

Fawkner wrote a typical editorial in his newspaper:

Citizens, rally round your Governor, let him see at once, that he is fortunate in being appointed to rule over a body of ardent, intelligent, persevering and enterprising men who have commenced a powerful colony, not only without Government assistance but who have gone on improving it, in defiance of all the impediments thrown in their way by the influence of rich and designing landed proprietors of Sydney who, to enhance the value of their lands, in the near neighbourhood of that capital, have done their utmost to ruin Port Phillip. We want no help, we want only to be permitted to use our own funds, our own resources and under our talented Lieutenant Governor we boldly say we will soon eclipse the present seat of Government.

Not even the optimistic Johnny Fawkner, knowing full well that he had promoted the Superintendent to Governor and the district to a colony, could have guessed how accurately he prophesied. In 1840, the sale of Crown Lands alone produced almost a quarter of a million pounds. Even so, the pioneers continued to complain bitterly that twenty-five-acre blocks were being offered for sale in the rapidly developing suburbs, inviting speculation by shrewd sub-dividers. Several land sales were held in Sydney, 600 miles away, so that absentee speculators made huge profits because local residents were willing to buy at almost any price.

Just as Melbourne appeared to be settling down to an assured future, a series of bankruptcies shattered confidence. Money had been advanced for speculative ventures, and farmers in the Western district and an increasingly large number of overlanders from New South Wales, had borrowed funds to stock large holdings. When the demand for sheep slackened, the whole community was involved. Imports fell; importation of beer and spirits dropped from 650,000 to 120,000 gallons a year. A smug local wrote that 'this shows how sincere our efforts have been.' The year was 1842, the population 8,000, and the first elections of the Town of Melbourne were about to be held. Soon afterwards the Port Phillip District (Victoria) was granted representation in the new Legislative Council of New South Wales.

But the desire for independence grew when Sydney decided that several hundred specially chosen 'exiles' should be landed in Port Phillip District. The men were prisoners who had earned, by good conduct, remission of their sentences on condition that they did not return to England until their term expired. Although the city dwellers hated them, many squatters and graziers who were short of labour welcomed them, and so widened the gulf between town and country.

Yet another petition for separation was sent to Queen Victoria. La Trobe, while he favoured separation, considered the people too inexperienced to govern themselves. He became so unpopular that Queen Victoria received a petition to recall him. She refused. However, by 1848, with the news that Melbourne was to be proclaimed a city, it became fairly obvious that separation from New South Wales could not be long delayed. On 4 April 1849, a special meeting of the Privy Council attended by the Queen at Buckingham Palace, discussed only one item, the separation of the Port Phillip District. On 5 August the necessary Bill was passed by the British House of Commons and was later given Royal Assent.

Before separation was implemented, Victorians had another opportunity to show their attitude to Sydney. In 1849, it was announced that the Randolph was arriving with convicts despite the promise of the Governor of New South Wales, Sir Charles Fitzroy, that none would be sent. Meetings were called and violent speeches made. La Trobe was warned that if any attempt was made to land the convicts, they would be repulsed by force.

Creswick's Creek, from Spring Hill.

Published by Sands & Kenny, Melbourne & Sydney, 1857.

The Randolph *was sent on, as was the* Hashemy, *a second convict ship.*

On the heels of Victoria's independence came the announcement of the gold discoveries. Money and men soon began pouring into Britain's newest colony. The first miners came from New South Wales and South Australia.

Among these diggers was a slim, thirty-four year old red-bearded painter of medium height, Samuel Thomas Gill, who was to become the only commercially successful artist of the gold-rush period, and whose fame and fortune was to last just about as long as the gold rush itself. He was to die a pauper in 1880, aged sixty-two—although his age on a headstone erected by public subscription is incorrectly shown as sixty.

As his work was rediscovered and interest in him as an artist revived, research revealed that he was born at Perriton, Somerset, on 21 May 1818, the son of the Rev. Samuel Gill, headmaster of a Plymouth school and brother to a member of the House of Commons. Young Samuel apparently had drawing lessons from his father, and at one stage worked in London for the Hubard Profile Gallery which sold silhouettes.

In 1839 Gill migrated to South Australia with his parents to settle in the lovely Coromandel Valley near Adelaide, where his father built a commodious house whose kitchen was large enough to be used as a church. By 1843, the Rev. Samuel was advertising that he would undertake the education of a limited number of 'young gentlemen under twelve years of age' whose instruction would include 'Writing and Arithmetic; The English, Latin and Greek grammars; Instruction in the Arts and Sciences; Geography, History and the laying of a Classical Education.' The fees were £20 for board and instruction, and £2 each for mending and washing.

The younger Samuel had also burst into print. In March 1840 he opened a studio in Gawler Place Adelaide. He described himself as an artist, 'late Draughtsman and Water Colour Painter to the Hubard Profile Gallery of London . . . who solicits the attendance of such individuals as are desirous of obtaining likenesses of themselves, families and friends.' Later in the advertisement he said that 'correct resemblances of horses, dogs and local scenery will be executed to order . . .'

Two of his earliest works show the departure of the famous explorer Charles Sturt from Adelaide in 1844. Two years later, Gill himself set off as an unpaid draughtsman on an expedition organised by a local explorer, J. A. Horrocks, during which he kept a diary that underlined his love for painting. Horrocks, in his journal, confirms this devotion and records that the progress of the expedition was occasionally held up while Gill sketched. When Horrocks accidentally but fatally wounded himself, Gill showed himself a sympathetic companion and friend who made the last hours of his friend as restful as possible. Earlier Horrocks had discovered and named Lake Gill (Lake Dutton) after his friend.

When Gill returned to Adelaide, so little was thought of his drawings that he had to raffle them. From the records available, it appears that the explorer Sturt may have held a few lucky tickets because he presented several of these sketches to Queen Victoria when he visited England shortly afterwards. Four of them were returned by Queen Elizabeth to the Commonwealth and now hang in the National Library, Canberra.

In 1845 Gill is said to have imported the equipment for making daguerreotypes, but whether he ever produced any work is not known. Two years later he organized Adelaide's first 'Artists' Exhibition'. His bush scenes attracted a lot of attention, though a local critic complained that they lacked contrast and were 'rather too thin and wanting in effect'. In that year also, at least two, possibly three, hand-coloured lithographs by Gill were published in George French Angas's South Australia Illustrated. One of them was based on his 1844 drawings of the departure of Sturt's expedition. Throughout the 1840s Gill also drew many suburban and rural scenes around Adelaide and the surrounding hills.

On 31 May 1849 the South Australian Gazette reported that 'twelve lithographic sketches of colonists—all pretty well known—have been published during the week under the title 'Heads of the People'. They are from the pencil of Mr Gill and show that the ability of this artist is not confined to landscape drawing but that it extends to a branch of art hitherto unexplored by him. These sketches are for the most part well done, one or two of them inimitable; and there is just that spice of quiet humour, bordering upon caricature, which redeems them from the dull monotony of staring portraits, without the slightest offence to the individuals introduced.' In all, twenty-two lithographed drawings were published in this series. Gill drew them on the lithographer's stone and they were said to be excellent likenesses. Before he left Adelaide at least two other lithographs—Old Colonists' Festival Dinner and Merry Monarch, a drawing of a racehorse—were published there.

But it was after his arrival on the Victorian goldfields in 1852 that Gill's sketches and drawings really began to attract attention. In that year fifty of them decorated the vestibule of the Theatre Royal, Bourke Street, Melbourne where Gill later became a regular patron at the bar. The thirteen years that followed produced nine volumes of sketches about life in the Victoria of the gold rushes. The first—A Series of Sketches of the Victorian Gold Diggings and Diggers as they are which contained twenty-four sketches lithographed and published in 1852 by Macartney & Galbraith of 30 Collins Street West—was among the best.

In February 1853, Gill exhibited some water-colours made from sketches done while he was with the Horrocks expedition and later that year his Views in and around Melbourne were in great demand in the city. In 1853 also, a set of coloured plates of his goldfield pictures was issued by H. H. Collins & Co. of London at the impressive price, for that time, of half a guinea. Some further proof of his appeal was the appearance on the English market of imitations of his work.

These years, 1853 to 1857, were among his most productive. The Diggers and Diggings of Victoria appeared in 1855 and his letter-paper headings with drawings were the forerunners of the modern picture postcard. At this time he often worked in a room above the shop of J. J. Blundell & Co., booksellers and publishers, in Collins Street, and was extraordinarily expert in transferring his designs directly on to the lithographic stone, using a glass to achieve the necessary reversals. These stones were then sent to Campbell & Fergusson's workshop a few doors away, where the prints were made and returned to Blundell. At this time also, Gill made a trip to New South Wales to draw.

View on the Yarra near Dights' Mill.

Published by Sands & Kenny, Melbourne & Sydney 1857

16 *His* Scenery in and around Sydney *was published in 1856, and the following year the first volume of* Victoria Illustrated *was published in Melbourne in an elaborate edition. In 1859 some of his coloured lithographs were published in Edward Wilson's* Rambles at the Antipodes.

His last and probably most famous collection of drawings appeared in 1865 in The Australian Sketchbook, *a portfolio of lithographed views. He still had a studio in Spring Street a year later, and was often seen in the company of Marcus Clarke and his friends. By now, his best work had been done, but happily the Public Library of Victoria in 1869 had the forethought to commission him to do a collection of forty paintings on life in the goldfields in 1852 and 1853. Apart from this work, he was content to sketch for a few shillings so that he could drink at his favourite bars at the Royal, the Cafe de Paris or Stutt's Buffet. His principal customers were hotelkeepers.*

The work of Gill has often been compared to the great English draughtsman and cartoonist, Thomas Rowlandson, who occupies an important place in English humorous art and caricature. But Rowlandson could be coarse in a way that was foreign to Gill, who preferred to laugh with rather than at his subjects. The superb First Subscription Ball, Ballarat, 1854 *completely captures the mood of people being silly enough to enjoy themselves thoroughly without any thought of the consequences.*

Gill had almost been forgotten by Melbourne people by the time of his death in 1880. But his work gradually became better known, probably by means of reproductions which appeared for sale in many bookshops about 1913, when the Victorian Historical Society began appealing for funds to remove his body from a pauper's grave. By 1945 Gill was described by Bernard Smith in Place, Taste and Tradition *as 'the most important artist of the goldfields, the most significant artist between Martens and Buvelot, and the most Australian of all artists'. This enthusiasm for his goldfields sketches has overshadowed the ability shown in drawings of the kind chosen for inclusion in this book. His skill as a draughtsman and illustrator can be appreciated if a magnifying glass is used to study the extraordinary detail he managed to include.*

Gill's last commission was given to him by his friend, Arthur Peck, who wanted Gill to add some embellishments to the perspective of a building that Peck was planning. The artist's hands were shaking so much—he had a habit in later years of holding a wrist with the other hand to steady it—that Peck sent him off until the following day.

To the end, Gill enjoyed the help of a few friends who saw to it that he received lodgings and a bed. He had never been a recluse, he liked company and always retained a certain air of decayed gentility, even if, to strangers, his dignity was a little theatrical. However, on the day he died an old acquaintance who met him shuffling along recalled that he spoke haltingly and incoherently. On 27 October 1880 Gill stumbled, fell and died on the steps of the G.P.O., Elizabeth Street; he had been, it is said, discussing the trial of the bushranger Ned Kelly then taking place in Melbourne. An inquest held the following day found the cause of death to be 'rupture of an aneurism of the aorta'.

He was buried in a public grave marked only by a small metal tag. The new headstone over his grave, which stands a little to the west of the graves of the explorers Burke and Wills in the Melbourne General Cemetery, carries the following inscription:

Samuel Thomas Gill
The Artist of the Goldfields
Died in Melbourne, October 27th, 1880
Aged 60 years
Erected by the Historical Society of Victoria, October 1913

LIST OF ILLUSTRATIONS

BALLAARAT POST OFFICE AND TOWNSHIP FROM GOVERNMENT ENCLOSURE

In 1857, this location (later the site of the Railway Hotel, Lydiard Street, Ballarat) was the centre of what was then one of the most famous cities in the world. Six years earlier gold had been found at Poverty Point, and there were other dramatic successes: James Esmond won £2,000 worth of gold in a couple of days, the Cavanagh brothers literally picked up nuggets worth £2,100 in an afternoon, and Howe and Herring were richer by £1,800 after four hours of digging.

By 1854, 319,154 ounces of gold worth a million pounds had been sent to Melbourne under police escort. In the next four years more than two and a half million ounces worth £10,000,000 were sent. Probably many more millions went out of the district in the boxes, bags and goldbelts of the miners. No wonder poets broke into verse.

> *Ho! Ho! Have ye heard of Ballarat?*
> *Then bid farewell and sail away,*
> *Sail and sail for a hundred day,*
> *Across the seas to Hobson's Bay,*
> *To the golden fields of Ballarat.*

Many diggers were disappointed, but often they were those with little mining experience. Others from Cornwall and Wales, skilled in tin and copper mining, banded together in groups. Striking shafts fifty and sixty feet down. They searched successfully in the leads or underground gutters where more gold was concentrated. These men had their horse-drawn whims and whips, their puddlers and, later on, their stationary steam engines to work the ground economically.

A new phase began in the mid-1850s with the discovery of gold in quartz reefs. By 1860, thousands of miners and even more shareholders and speculators were making a good living from more than fifty quartz mines which used hundreds of stampers to separate gold from the stone. The 'Star of the East' alone had a hundred battery stampers. It employed not only miners, engine drivers and carters, but, with other mines, helped to keep a hundred sharebrokers busy on the local Mining Exchange. The 'Welcome Nugget' was discovered on 9 June 1858 at a depth of 180 feet at Bakery Hill. It contained almost a hundredweight and a half of pure gold, was sold for £10,500, and was exhibited at the Crystal Palace in London for several months before being turned into sovereigns.

But in December 1854 the Eureka Stockade became a part of history. Miners had been regularly harassed by police to pay a mining licence. They built their stockade enclosing an acre where they began drilling with guns and even pikes. A thousand tense miners were there on Friday 1 December but by Sunday morning 3 December only about one hundred and fifty men remained to fight briefly and vainly against the attack of four hundred troops and police. Five soldiers were killed, thirty miners were killed or later died of wounds. After Eureka the miners were given the vote, their leader Peter Lalor became their first member of Parliament, the licence was abolished and the government appointed a commission to inquire into conditions on the goldfields.

Golden Ballarat lasted until about 1870, when a slump forced population down from 50,000 to 38,000. The newly created city was in such financial difficulties that the clock in the city hall was not lit at night, many of the streets were in darkness and the works programmes were drastically reduced. Gradually Ballarat, whose goldfields had yielded more than 20,000,000 ounces, or 630 tons, of gold worth £230,000,000, replaced large-scale mining with other industries and became an important provincial centre.

STATIONERS T & W BROWN POST OFFICE

Ballaarat Post Office & Township, from Government Enclosure.

Published by Sands & Kenny, Melbourne & Sydney, 185

LYDIART ST. FROM BATH'S HOTEL, BALLAARAT

Early in 1852, the Victorian government sent surveyor W. H. Urquhart to Ballarat to lay out a township. He decided that the main official street with public offices, churches, banks and hotels should be named Lydiard Street (not Lydiart Street as the original caption has it) after John Charles Pitfield Lydiard, the escort officer-in-charge of the native police who in the first few months regularly convoyed the gold from Ballarat to Melbourne.

Many Ballarat miners and tradesmen resented Urquhart's plans. From the first, he had decided that the low-lying but popular Main Road was an unsuitable location. Later events proved him right, but for about ten years Main Road provided strong opposition to the official township. In the late fifties and early sixties, the block between Eureka and Esmond (now York) Streets contained sixty shops, twelve hotels and four well-equipped theatres, none of which closed much before midnight. Meantime as the drawing shows Lydiard Street was achieving the purpose Urquhart had for it. The intersection is Sturt Street, with the government enclosure on the right-hand side. The surveyor had first considered a high spot near the present junction of Humffray and Grant Streets, but ultimately decided upon moving to the plateau out of the populated areas.

The first Municipal Council of Ballarat, with James Oddie as Chairman, met on 5 May 1857 in the Golden Fleece Hotel. A little later that year a rival municipal council was formed in Ballarat East, or The Flat as it was often called in opposition to The Township on the plateau. For more than sixty years, attempts were made to bring the two councils together. Early in 1860 there seemed some hope that the two councils might amalgamate when a disastrous fire destroyed both sides of the busy Main Street block between Eureka and York Streets. Other fires and several floods forced many merchants to move to the higher area where Sturt Street gradually became the business centre. With Main Street slowly losing its importance, it was thought that the East Ballarat Council would favour one council, but although the ratepayers voted four times, they refused amalgamation. Not until the First World War brought the two councils together was another attempt made. They became one on 15 May 1921, and the old enmity between The Flat and The Township became a memory.

What had probably strengthened East Ballarat's determination to remain independent was that until 1856 all mining was concentrated in their area. But in that year some of the smaller co-operative groups which had been working deeper shafts decided to move up to the plateau above Lydiard Street. There they blasted with gunpowder, sometimes through three and four hundred feet of heavy stone, to find the leads again underneath. Their first success came at the corner of Sturt and Lydiard Streets, at Bath's Freehold. Soon dozens of similar mines were opened in what are now the City's main streets. Both sides of Dana, Eyre, Urquhart and South Streets were lined with mines between Albert and Pleasant Streets. Other groups opened up in Drummond Street and around Lake Wendouree, while streets off Sturt Street, including Lydiard, provided their excitement. The most successful mines were the Cosmopolitan in Dana Street (named after Lydiard's old commandant of the Native Police Force) which produced £161,000, and the Kohinoor in Urquhart Street yielding £681,000.

The description of Ballarat as 'a city built on gold' was thus not just a figure of speech.

Lydiart St. from Baths Hotel, Ballaarat.

Published by Sands & Kenny. Melbourne & Sydney. 1857.

22 *The Melbourne* Argus *of September 1851 carried the following letter:*

Dear Sir,

I wish to publish these few lines in your valuable paper that the public may know that there is gold found in these ranges about 4 miles from Dr Barker's home station, and about a mile from the Melbourne road, at the southernmost point of Mount Alexander [Castlemaine], where three men and myself are working. I do this to prevent parties getting us into trouble as we have been threatened to have the constables fetched for being on the ground. If you will have the kindness to insert this in your paper, we will be prepared to pay anything that is just, when the Commissioner comes. In the name of the party, John Worley, Mount Alexander Ranges, September 1st, 1851.

Within three months of this announcement, more than 8,000 men were digging feverishly on the Mount Alexander goldfields; in another three months there were 25,000. The Commissioner (later Chief Commissioner) Wright faced an almost insuperable task. Miners often waited for hours to get their licences and resented continual nagging and searching by police, many of them ex-convicts from Tasmania. Tension also arose from the gradual invasion of the fields by Chinese, who comprised a quarter of the goldfield population by 1855 and a half by 1861.

Commissioner Wright established his headquarters at the junction of Forest and Barker's Creeks where a flag in this engraving marks the location of his Camp Reserve, now the home of the Castlemaine Football Club. By the end of 1851 almost 100,000 ounces of gold had been escorted to Melbourne. In one convoy which left the Commissioner's office in July 1852, seven drays, escorted by seventeen foot soldiers and six troopers, carried 83,592 ounces—almost three tons—to Melbourne. By 1861, more than three and a half million ounces worth £14,000,000 had come out of the Mount Alexander goldfields. The town—named Castlemaine by Wright after his uncle, Lord Castlemaine an Irish peer—boomed, but the officials in their camp often lived on far better food and drink than was available elsewhere. The townspeople resented the 'campites' who controlled the settlement. But the formation of the Castlemaine Municipal Council ended their rule in 1855, although it was not forgotten by men like William Hiscock who wrote in 1856: 'Those of you who looked upon this Camp Scene a short time ago beheld it revelling in cruelty, dissipation, partiality, injustice and other enormities.'

Such criticism was justified in that half the proceeds of fines for sly grogging and evasion of licence fees were going to the policemen concerned. Gold Commissioners like C. Rudston Read admitted that some policemen neglected their normal duties to make money by blackmail and perjury. One police superintendent was thought to have made a fortune of £15,000 before he retired. He was in the habit of burning down offenders' tents, slashing with a whip, and protecting sly grog sellers. But in general only a few of the Commissioners' officers were corrupt. Most were hated rather for their haughty manners and snobbish attitude.

Fortunately the miners were led by men who believed in tolerance, who felt that any violence would ruin their just cause, and often feared that Americans on the goldfields might advocate lynch law. The wonder of the Australian goldfields is that there should have persisted such a deep-seated respect for authority when at many places, particularly Castlemaine, there was little enough reason for it.

Forest Creek, from Road to Castlemaine.

Published by Sands & Kenny Melbourne & Sydney. 1857.

MARKET SQUARE, CASTLEMAINE

This engraving emphasises how early the township of Castlemaine had taken on an air of permanence, for the view is the same, as far as buildings are concerned, as the one Gill made in 1855, only four years after gold was found. From 1851, although there was a constant ebb and flow of miners to new gold rushes, Castlemaine attracted great crowds. By June 1854 about 34,000 men were digging there.

By 1857 the value of the buildings and property in the township centred on this Market Square exceeded £200,000, and the editor of the local paper, the Mount Alexander Mail, *gave his readers a vision of the city as he believed it would be in 1887:*

The census returns just published exhibit the gratifying fact that the population of this city and its suburbs falls very little short of 250,000 souls . . . Castlemaine still maintains its place as second only to the metropolis of Victoria . . . the cathedrals, public library, college, parks and promenades, all bespeak the opulence of our population and bear eloquent testimony to the rapidity of our progress.

The vision soon faded. Although the population had risen to 29,000 in 1858, it then gradually dropped to about 7,000 in modern times. It remains a lovely city with many reminders of its golden past.

The two-storey building in the left background is the present A.N.Z. Bank. The Hall of Castlemaine on the left, was replaced by the Royal Theatre, which includes part of the original building built by William Hiscock in 1853 and advertised in the Mount Alexander Mail *of 6 May 1854 as:*

'HALL OF CASTLEMAINE. *Public Amusements, Public Meetings, Concerts, etc. The Hall of Castlemaine, 50 × 100 feet, with suitable fittings and arrangements, is to be let, for the evening, or by the week. Terms £10 per night, or £50 per week, including lighting and the attendance and services of six hall porters.'*

Soon afterwards, William Westgarth, parliamentarian and member of a government commission of inquiry on the goldfields, was writing that canvas roofs and walls were gradually disappearing and wood and stone were being used for more permanent buildings. A young English wife who had lived in a 'tent house' for two years went to a tea party in the new home of a friend. 'While loaded pistols decorated the mantelpiece,' she says, 'I found the women elegantly dressed in the latest fashion.'

The health of Castlemaine's people was a grave problem. 'Rheumatism is beginning to be very prevalent . . . dysentery too is exceedingly common all over the diggings, from the impurity of the water one is obliged to drink . . . there have been a great many deaths': so runs a diary of 1852. The death-rate among children was very high, probably due to drinking local water. 'The present water supply is from an insignificant and intermittent creek . . .', complains the Council in 1856, 'which . . . for miles . . . is the sole sewer and repository for filth of an extensive population, which office it has also to perform here.'

In 1856, William Hiscock was condemning the 'dismal and horribly thronged gaol' of which a prisoner had earlier written: 'I am confined in a log building twelve feet by twelve feet. Seventeen slept here the first night, twenty-eight the second, and twenty the third. The bedding is not allowed to be aired and the vermin is intolerable.' That building has disappeared, but two nearby trees to which prisoners were chained when the gaol was full long survived it.

EARTHENWARE AND GLASSWARE

HALL&POASTLEMAINE

Market Square, Castlemaine.

Published by Sands & Kenny, Melbourne & Sydney, 1857.

SPRING HILL FROM ROAD TO GOVERNMENT CAMP, CRESWICK'S CREEK

Spring Hill was one of many rounded hills rising from rich volcanic plains around what is now Creswick, fifteen miles north of Ballarat. Although Alfred Selwyn, a former government geologist, had maintained that gold lay buried below the basalt bedrock, it was not until 1872 that his prediction was proved correct. Until then most of the gold mining in Creswick had been alluvial, with men working claims ten feet by ten feet, digging out the pay dirt for washing or winding up buckets of earth filled by their mates below. While men raced from one new field to another, often leaving a fortune behind them, many stayed at Creswick because work there was easier and one could work on one's own or with a few mates. So the alluvial diggings attracted the inexperienced, 'the distinguished foreigners, broken down gentlemen and others incapable of the labour and perseverance necessary to any chance of success at the deep sinkings of Ballarat.'

'Well it don't suit me', said Tim, 'I'm sure;
That crowbar makes my hands too sore
And miserably soaked all day I've stood
Rocking the cradle knee deep in mud.
Now mucking at cooking, and slushing all day:
Now delving through dirty rocks and clay.
Gold digger! bah, it's all my eye . . .'

But a discovery near this hill completely changed the district's character by introducing large companies, expensive equipment, many wage earners, shareholders, brokers and speculators—and two very lucky men, Martin Loughlin and William (Weeping) Bailey.

After investigating new shafts in local wheatfields, Loughlin and Bailey formed a syndicate of eight Creswick and Ballarat men who bought 6,000 acres for £36,000. Loughlin and Bailey had already made a fortune out of the Mount Egerton mine which Bailey had managed for the Learmonths. Bailey's unenthusiastic reports ultimately persuaded his employers to sell the mine to Loughlin for £13,500. His employers paid Bailey as a faithful steward £675, a commission of five per cent on the sale. They were astonished to discover shortly afterwards that the mine was paying handsomely and that Bailey had a quarter share which in the first two and a half months, returned £30,000. Legal action was taken out but judgment was given for the defendants. When the Learmonths gained permission to appeal to the Privy Council, the matter was settled out of court.

Perhaps the smart, handsome, wavy-haired Loughlin and the tall, bearded, grave Bailey had just been lucky in the Mount Egerton deal, for they were certainly lucky in the years that followed. The Seven Hills estate was split up into areas and strips, which were offered to promoters and companies on the basis of a $7\frac{1}{2}$ per cent royalty on all gold found. In addition the two men helped to float companies like the West Ristori which struck gold and paid out £85,000; the Madame Ristori which produced £232,000; the Lone Hand, £283,000; the Berry Consols, £393,000; and the Loughlin, £70,000. The richest was the Madame Berry, sixth among the fourteen gold mines in Victoria which produced more than one million pounds worth of gold. Its proven output of 387,314 ounces was worth £1,588,515.

In all, the Seven Hills mines paid out £2,000,000 in profits. Bailey built a magnificent house costing £14,000 in Ballarat; it was completed in 1888 and sold in 1915 to the Catholic Church; it became part of the St John of God Hospital. Loughlin lived richly at the Esplanade Hotel in St Kilda. Both men raced horses which won two Victoria Derbys for Bailey and a Melbourne Cup for Loughlin.

To explain the nickname 'Weeping' Bailey some historians say he wept when given the commission cheque for the sale of Mt Egerton; others that the tears came when the Learmonths accused him of fraud.

Spring Hill, from Road to Government Camp, Creswick's Creek.

Published by Sands & Kenny, Melbourne & Sydney. 1857.

GOVERNMENT CAMP, CRESWICK'S CREEK

On 15 August 1851 Governor La Trobe announced that all gold found in Victoria, whether on private or Crown lands, was the property of the Queen and that any person who disturbed the soil in search for gold, without Government authority, would be liable to prosecution. A little later, licences to dig were issued and local Commissioners were appointed to control various goldfields.

These Commissioners usually set up their camps, as at Creswick, on high ground to give them useful vantage points. The first Commissioner in Creswick's Creek—now known as Creswick and named after the original squatting station established in 1842 by Henry and John Creswick—chose his so that, in addition, he could see the gold escort fording the creek on its way to Ballarat fifteen miles away. Gold and bushrangers went together, and bushrangers such as Captain Melville and 'Black' Douglas were later part of the history of Creswick and the surrounding district.

Lieutenant Charles Blackenbury, the first Commissioner, had served with the East India Company. He was tall and well built, a fine horseman and a capable boxer, and was determined that his escort should not be robbed. Under his command was sub-inspector John Charles Lydiard, whose name was given to an important street in Ballarat. Lydiard, jocularly called 'Lightheart', was a capable and respected officer who taught his mounted troopers to recognise the importance of their escort duties. The gold went to Ballarat weekly in sealed canvas bags strapped across the saddle of a pack-horse led by a trooper. On one side rode Lydiard, on the other a corporal, and behind three troopers. This escort was never robbed.

Gold had been discovered in the Creswick District in September 1851; a government select commission had awarded £580 to J. P. Main and eleven others as reward money for finding a payable goldfield. By 1854 the first quarter-acre blocks in the township were offered for sale after a survey in August of that year, and the one long street of the diggings was soon bustling with miners and local entertainments which included two hotels and a good theatre. Advertisements nailed on trees reminded patrons that the best seats were five shillings, with second-class ones at two and sixpence.

By this time Ballarat miners had begun their fight against the licence system. Their delegates visited the miners of Creswick to remind them that they suffered from the same injustices.

Moral persuasion is all a humbug,
Nothing convinces like a lick in the lug.

So, on Thursday 30 November 1854, three or four hundred Creswick miners gathered behind their best-known grog shanty. Headed by a German band playing the Marseillaise, and carrying firearms, crowbars, pick handles and anything else useful for administering 'a lick in the lug', they set off for Ballarat. It was hot and dusty, and a sudden and violent thunderstorm made the marchers break ranks, most of them returning to Creswick. Next day two hundred set off again.

It has been plausibly suggested that these two aggressive actions may have precipitated the action that was taken against the Ballarat miners at Eureka. Authority may have felt that, if neighbouring miners were going to add their strength to that of the Ballarat revolutionaries, the sooner the matter was settled the better.

As it turned out, the Creswick miners took no further part in the events culminating in the Eureka Stockade. But Creswick miners have a place in trade union history. In 1883, after the worst accident in Australian gold mining history, in which twenty-two men died at Creswick, William Spence revived the Amalgamated Miners' Association of Victoria. With 7,000 members, it was Australia's largest trade union. The first president was John Sampson, a practical miner of high integrity, and grandfather of a Prime Minister, Sir Robert Menzies.

Government Camp, Creswick's Creek.

Published by Sands & Kenny, Melbourne & Sydney, &c.

MOUNT MACEDON FROM LAGOON N. OF BUSH INN

The 'Shipping Intelligence' of the Melbourne Argus of 22 March 1852 contained this announcement:

Arrived, Amazon, barque, 400 tons, from Adelaide. Passengers: (Cabin) Lord Robert Cecil, Sir Montague Chapman, Mr Turner and lady, Mr Jones, Dr Wright, and 150 in the steerage.

Aged twenty-two, Lord Cecil belonged to one of England's most distinguished families. He was later to be thrice Prime Minister of Britain as Lord Salisbury. He had been advised to take a long sea journey to recuperate from arduous university studies. While in Capetown the Irish baronet Chapman, persuaded him to see something of the Victorian goldfields on his way to New Zealand.

The day after their arrival in Melbourne, Lord Cecil and Chapman were in a spring cart on this road to the Mt Alexander (Castlemaine) diggings. Like the five other passengers they were bounced about on the rough road; the jolts brought screams from the only woman traveller. 'We stopped several times at coffee shops, the euphonious name, generally speaking, for sly grog shops', says the noble lord in his diary, parts of which were later published. 'I was struck at these places by the perfect civility with which everyone treated us.' This comment seems justified, for, although the Bush Inn at Gisborne was crowded and all the other passengers were refused admission, the two bluebloods were allowed in on the strength of their black coats. What the other passengers said about the civility of hotelkeepers was not recorded.

In the same year, another engaging traveller Mrs Charles Clacy, recorded that the Bush Inn was 'a large, well-built, brick and weatherboard house with bedrooms for private families'. Mrs Clacy said that the hotel boasted a detached weatherboard and stone kitchen with tap room and sleeping lofts, part of which, with the accompanying stabling, was set aside for the police gold escorts. She remarked that a New Bush Inn was also available to travellers but that 'the charges at these houses are enormous. Five and six shillings for a meal, seven and sixpence for a bottle of ale, and one shilling for half a glass or nobbler of brandy.'

The Bush Inn was on the present site of the post office in Gisborne and had been opened in 1840. It was a favourite spot for the second night's stopover from Melbourne on the way to the goldfields; here even early in the morning, people took a little dutch courage before they set out on the road past Mount Macedon and through the Black Forest, noted for its bushrangers.

The small group of huts and buildings around the Bush Inn became known as Bush Town, and it was here that Henry Gisborne, the police commissioner of Port Phillip (west side), set up his barracks, gaol, residence, store rooms and horse paddocks. When Gisborne died—he was only twenty-six—Governor La Trobe renamed the place Gisborne. Later, as the drawing indicates, the road between Gisborne and Woodend was much improved; the lagoon named Wright's Lagoon was drained and became a race-course. It was closed some thirty years ago because it was too wet. The Bush Inn closed in 1863 after the opening of the Melbourne-Bendigo railway.

With few exceptions the Victorian gold fields were at least sixty to seventy miles from Melbourne. So, for a time at least, the production of wealth in Victoria was decentralised. This produced better communications; immense sums—for the period—were spent on road and rail systems which gave employment to tens of thousands.

Mount Macedon, from Lagoon N. of Bush Inn.

Published by Sands & Kenny, Melbourne & Sydney, 1857.

32   *In 1851 an earlier bridge at Keilor built of logs was carried away by floodwaters but a punt had replaced it within two months. However, the banks were steep, the stream narrow and rapid, and the punt-keeper was often drunk and incapable. Travellers had then to ford the river; sometimes their horses were swept downstream several hundred yards. The charges when the ferry was working were sixpence for a passenger, a shilling for a horse or bullock, one and sixpence for a two-wheeled vehicle and two shillings for a loaded dray.*

The keeper's condition permitting, the punt was worked from six in the morning until half past six at night and was available at double rates outside those hours. 'However,' continues the diarist Mrs Charles Clacy, 'this road to the diggings [at Castlemaine and Bendigo] is not much used.' This changed soon afterwards. The acting Colonial Engineer, Samuel Brees, requested money for the increasingly busy road to Keilor. When work began with 650 men working a twelve-hour day from six o'clock in the morning for ten shillings Brees was granted police escorts and guards for the paymasters. Brees also designed the bridge shown in this drawing. The original estimate was £7,816 but the scarcity of labour lifted all expenses and by the time the bridge was completed in 1854 it had cost £20,000.

The small weatherboard building of two rooms sitting against the bridge was the Keilor Toll House, a fruitful source of income, particularly in the fifties when it was reckoned that £500 a month was collected. Tolls ranged from as little as a farthing for a sheep, pig or goat, a penny for cattle and threepence for a horse or ass, to varying amounts for vehicles, depending on the number of animals drawing them; sixpence was charged for each horse or ox. There was a cheaper rate for broad-wheeled tyres, on the basis that they did less damage. Most travellers hated tolls, but the revenue was important to shires and municipalities who otherwise would have had to increase local rates to maintain trunk roads used by through traffic. By 1871, the revenue had dropped off considerably—only £480 for the year—particularly with the introduction of the Melbourne-Bendigo railway. In 1877 the toll gate was abolished.

During the golden years this Keilor road must have been fascinating. It saw the fierce competition between Cobb & Co. coaches, often called the Yankee Line, and the locally-owned line run by Foster. Journeys often took on the excitement of a blue-ribbon steeplechase. 'We had one effective specimen of road racing beyond Essendon,' says a diarist, 'during which the tops of the coaches often came into collision and a tall gentleman in the mail had his head driven clean through the closed leather roof by a violent bump.' But this was only the beginning of a memorable day for the diarist. The first stop was at Keilor where the traveller hoped to get breakfast. The huge juicy steak he had ordered apparently never reached the table but was grabbed, with its platter, on the journey between kitchen and dining room.

In 1852, a visitor described Keilor as 'a pretty little village with a good inn, several nice cottages and a store or two'. A hundred years later it had not greatly changed; the population was only 3,243 in 1947. Today it has become one of the fastest-growing areas in Australia.

Township of Keilor from South side of Bridge.

Published by Sands & Kenny Melbourne & Sydney 1857.

SANDHURST

As early as 1857, Sandhurst (Bendigo) was already giving signs that it would become an important provincial city. Town allotments were in demand; between £30 and £50 a foot was paid for sites in Pall Mall, the main street. A number of one-storey buildings had replaced the temporary canvas structures and William Westgarth wrote in a government report about the amount of corrugated iron being used. He mentioned the Sandhurst Exhibition, and the variety of entertainment advertised on handbills nailed to posts and trees—two theatres, a circus and a variety theatre. He found the dinner excellent at the Bendigo Hotel and the wines good.

Showing the growing permanency of the settlement was the increasingly high proportion of females in the population: 3,294 out of a total 12,159. Visitors talked about the church parades of well-dressed men, women and children, and Westgarth records that 'the quietness of the diggings on a Sunday is striking. There seems to be a general agreement to cease from the usual occupation'.

Except for Sunday, which on all diggings was regarded as a day of rest, Bendigo had been a very different settlement four years earlier. It was here that many commentators of the day expected the trial of strength between miners and government over licence fees. Twenty thousand of the fifty thousand miners in Victoria were in Bendigo in 1853, and the highly-belligerent but well-controlled diggers' movement was highly organised. Government officials were lampooned and tree trunks carried posters reading 'No chains for free Englishmen'. The Anti-Gold-Licence Association offered a ten-guinea prize for the best essay on 'The Iniquity of the Gold Licence Tax'.

On 1 August 1853 a petition to Governor La Trobe asked that the licence fee be reduced to ten shillings, that armed forces leave the fields and that diggers be given the vote. Tempers became frayed at the meeting and the miners left, saying they would pay no more than ten shillings a month. In a giant rally in Bendigo on 13 August some 12,000 men strongly supported their leaders. 'Gully after gully hoisted its flag', wrote a Herald *reporter. 'The Germans had splendid new banners, the English had royal standards and Union Jacks, the Irish provided themselves with a beautiful flag with a harp supported by pick and shovel.'*

The testing day was 27 August. Hundreds of diggers and their leaders offered only ten shillings for their licence, and themselves for arrest. The police could do nothing except report that Bendigo was in a state of revolution. The government was powerless and in an amending Act agreed to a tax of £2 for the remaining four months of the year and to reduced taxes of £1, £2, £4 and £8 for periods of one, three, six and twelve months. 'The Government is humbled in the dust before a lawless mob' wrote The Times *in London. Governor La Trobe knew the weaknesses of the licence system which he had regarded as temporary only. In his official report to London, therefore, he suggested that republican influences were to blame, though whether American, Irish or Chartist was never made plain.*

Meantime the miners' other demands were politely pushed aside, and their mass support fell away. The miners' leaders were unable to form a State Diggers' Congress.

The government appeared to recognise, for the time being, that it could not successfully operate the licence system. Only about half the miners were paying the tax by May 1854 but the government made little effort to fine defaulters. So the insistence of the new governor, Sir Charles Hotham, on strong action to collect the licence fees surprised all miners. On top of that, official stupidity and brutality, as well as what the miners felt was a gross miscarriage of justice about the murder of a miner, made conditions ideal for the Eureka Stockade at Ballarat—not Bendigo.

GOV SALE
LAND

Sandhurst.

Published by Sands & Kenny, Melbourne & Sydney. 1857

PORT OF WARRNAMBOOL

When, on 2 July 1847, the government auctioneer G. S. Brodie, mounted his rostrum in rooms at the corner of Elizabeth and Little Collins Streets Melbourne, and began offering for sale 167 allotments of Crown lands, the city of Warrnambool was born. But interesting events spread over eleven years lay behind the auctions, which brought in more than £3,000.

Hugh Donnelly, who was in charge of the whaling station at Griffiths Island off Port Fairy, tells of three sealers, Smith, Gibbs and Wilson, who saw the Hopkins River as early as 1836 when their boat overturned in a heavy swell and Smith was drowned. Gibbs and Wilson struggled ashore and walked overland to Port Fairy. There they spoke so enthusiastically about the nearby islands, which were full of seals, that this area became a favourite hunting ground.

The discovery of rich farming land between Warrnambool and Port Fairy was also made from the sea. When survivors of the 255-ton barque Children—wrecked on 5 January 1839 at nearby Childers Cove—had to tramp to the nearest settlement, Port Fairy, they noticed the rich land. They reported to the government when they ultimately reached Sydney. Earlier, in 1836, the explorer Major (later Sir) Thomas Mitchell had described in glowing terms the well-watered and excellent grazing country in that part of the Western District. Finally, squatters further north in the colony, suffering from the severe droughts in the late 1830s, drove their stock down to the Warrnambool district.

Among the well-known squatters were the Manifolds, the Allans of Allandale, Mark Nicholson who came to Australia with the explorer Leichhardt, and Strong and Foster who in 1844 had the grazing rights over the present site of the city. In the winter of 1844 the schooner Osprey made two trips between Hobart Town and Warrnambool carrying fat cattle from the Allans' Tooram estate which they had occupied since 1839.

But it was seamen—not squatters or pastoralists—whose actions led to the foundation of Warrnambool. A boat's crew of the Adelaide discovered Warrnambool Bay while pursuing whales in August 1844. Later that year the mate of the Adelaide, A. McMillan, surveyed the bay, after which a memorial was sent to Governor La Trobe asking for an official inspection of the area. Among the seven memorialists was Charles Mills, one of the two famous Mills brothers of Port Fairy, and Captain Gay of the Adelaide. In 1846, Robert Hoddle and Lieutenant Pickering surveyed the township and in January of 1847 it was named Warrnambool, a corruption of the local Aboriginal name pronounced 'Warnimble'.

Seven months later the Clarence brought John H. Craig and G. Nichol who built the first hotel (the Warrnambool) at the corner of Banyan and Merri Streets; it was followed by another built by George Chisholm and his uncle, John Moffat Chisholm, one of the best-known merchants of Melbourne. Two hotels and stores in quick succession suggested rapid growth but the jealousy of nearby Port Fairy had to be reckoned with. The Port Fairy magistrate twice refused applications for licences for the hotels and only when Warrnambool got its own magistrates were the licences granted.

By 1850 Warrnambool's population was only 342, and a year later when gold was found, and every able-bodied man left the town for the diggings, possibly fewer than one hundred people were left. With the return of successful miners and the establishment in 1857 of a tramway to the quayside, the township developed and its port exported local produce— wheat, wool, meat and potatoes.

Like Port Fairy and Portland, Warrnambool had its share of tragic wrecks. Among them, according to some local historians, was the old schooner Enterprise that had brought Fawkner's party up the Yarra on 20 October 1835.

Port of Warrnambool.

Published by Sands & Kenny Melbourne & Sydney 1857.

BELFAST, PORT FAIRY

In an interesting book called Why Should Their Honor Fade? Olive Mills writes: 'We, the grandchildren of Charles Mills, claim that John and Charles Mills, who settled permanently in Victoria in 1826 and remained there until the death of Charles Mills in 1855 and of John Mills in 1877, should have the right of being recognised as Victoria's first settlers.'

Historians may argue about the claims of these two brothers, John and Charles, who were only eighteen and fourteen years of age when they found safe anchorage with their sealing cutter at Port Fairy in 1826, but no one will deny the fame they had in western Victoria as seamen. Both were phenomenally strong. John Mills, assisted only by an Aborigine, was said to have lifted a great ship's capstan weighing five hundredweight. Charles Mills could throw a harpoon farther than any other man on the west coast and, after his boat had been wrecked by a whale, swam two miles through boiling seas to get help for his two seamates left clinging to the wreckage. He frightened off two sharks on the way.

Both men were part of the life of Port Fairy for many years. Sons of Lieutenant Peter Mills who served under Captain William Bligh, and who was pilot and harbourmaster of Launceston, they had to help the family when their father died while they were young. By the time they reached Port Fairy they were supporting themselves. Charles ultimately mixed farming, sealing and whaling, but John stayed with the sea in a variety of commands including that of the 600-ton Scottish ship David Clark, which carried in 1839 the first migrants direct from Britain to Port Phillip. In 1851 he became harbourmaster and pilot of Port Fairy, where he settled in a well-built but unpretentious cottage in Gipps Street.

Some maintain that Port Fairy's first permanent settlers were two whalers, Raby and Penny, who built a whaling station there in 1834. But it is generally agreed that Port Fairy was discovered by Captain James Wishart on 25 April 1810. With a crew of two he was racing ahead of a fierce gale on the lookout for a sheltered bay when he crossed the bar and sailed up what is now the River Moyne. Delighted with the surroundings and the safe anchorage, he named the place Port Fairy after his small ship Fairy. The area became a centre for hunting whales and seals: crews from Tasmania and New South Wales established their stations on Griffiths Island, shown in the foreground of Gill's drawing, as well as on the mainland. In 1836 more than a hundred experienced whaling hands were working for the Henty brothers, the Griffiths brothers and the whaling firm of Hewett & Co.

A year earlier Lieutenant-Surveyor Wedge had been directed to report to the colonial government in Sydney on the settlement and to make recommendations about a harbour. His enthusiastic report induced a Sydney solicitor, James Atkinson, to apply for a grant of land—and he got it. Despite protests from officials and prominent people in Melbourne, Atkinson became the virtual owner of 5,120 acres of land where Port Fairy now stands. He renamed Port Fairy Belfast after his native city in Northern Ireland but in 1887 an Act of Parliament gave the town back its old name. Waiting for the value of land to rise, Atkinson held on to his grant and early settlers had to move into virgin bushlands.

Port Fairy became the virtual centre of the Western District trade and one of the busiest seaports in Australia. Great bullock trains rolled on to the wharves where wheat, potatoes, wool and meat were loaded into ships sailing direct to London.

At one time immigrant barracks housed settlers until they moved up-country or found jobs locally. Fast clipper ships filled the bay. With the coming of rail and road transport, the little port lost much of its importance. Today it is noted for its fishing which was, after all, the reason why it was founded.

Belfast, Port Fairy.

Published by Sands & Kenny, Melbourne & Sydney 1857.

PORTLAND FROM THE BAY

Into this bay, on the 19 November 1834, the schooner Thistle *brought Edward Henty, recognised as Victoria's first permanent settler. To welcome him was Captain William Dutton whose whaling station was based there, but who, like the many whalers and sealers along the coast, never regarded the land as his home. That Edward Henty meant to stay was clear. His cargo included the frame of a house, 2,500 bricks, thousands of feet of sawn timber, flooring boards and weatherboards, 18,000 shingles, several bullocks, cows and bulls, food, seeds and tools.*

For Edward Henty, whatever his other qualities, was a practical man. On one occasion he and three brothers who had followed him to settle here were—with the station hands and servants—in the middle of their morning service when a whale was sighted in the Bay. Without so much as an 'Amen', the men left to catch the whale and bring it ashore. The service was then taken up from the sentence in the Book of Common Prayer which the whale had interrupted.

It is difficult to imagine, as has been reported, that the Hentys lived nearly two years in Portland before Sydney officials knew of it. Many Tasmanians must have known where the Hentys were, for they had often talked about the possibilities of the extensive tracts of land across Bass Strait. Nevertheless, Thomas Mitchell was undoubtedly surprised when he came across the family after he had explored the rich grazing lands of the Western District of Victoria. He suspected that the Hentys were ex-convicts illegally squatting on the bayside while they worked the sea for whales. The Hentys thought Mitchell's group were bushrangers.

Happily neither side fired, and soon the Hentys' good rum and tobacco made Mitchell expansive about the superb grazing land some forty miles north of Portland. This was on 29 August 1836, and not many days later the Hentys were out making their selection from the land which was to give them wealth and influence. In 1853, Edward Henty had 'Burswood' built, a magnificent house on a slope overlooking the broad sweep of Portland Bay. When Edward died in 1878, this house was estimated to be worth £30,000 but it was sold during the depression of 1895 for £600. In this home, the founder of Portland lived in almost feudal style with a retinue of butlers, footmen, cooks, gardeners, grooms and coachmen. In 1857, Henty's architect drew up ambitious plans for a breakwater to protect the port from dangerous winds and tides. But it was not until a century later that, at a cost of £6,000,000, Portland was transformed into a fine deepwater port.

The town grew with the years, but the wealth created by the goldfields had little effect on it—with perhaps one rather curious exception. In an attempt to lessen Chinese immigration to the goldfields, a tax of £10 was levied on all Chinese landing in Victoria and ships were officially allowed to bring in only one Chinese for each ten tons burthen. One result was that in the first six months of 1857, 14,000 Chinese landed at Port Robe in South Australia near the Western border of Victoria, and then walked to the Victorian goldfields. The immense numbers defeated most of the law's attempts to stop them, but a large group that was arrested was given a two months' sentence which was spent in Portland turning the local wilderness of a reserve into a garden.

Edward Henty, the founder of Portland, lived only five years after moving to his Melbourne house, 'Offington', in St Kilda Road, near Commercial Road.

Portland from the Bay.

Published by Sands & Kenny, Melbourne & Sydney 1857

APPROACH TO RICHMOND FROM NORTH BANK OF YARRA YARRA

In the 1850s this was a particularly popular stretch of the river Yarra although there were complaints about the many river steamers that ran from Melbourne to the Cremorne Gardens, near where Cremorne Street, Richmond is today. The gardens had been taken over by G. V. Brooke the well-known English actor, and George Coppin, entrepreneur and actor. Brooke and Coppin were said to have spent £100,000 creating a wonderland of attractions, and the Upper Yarra Steam Gondola Company carried thousands of pleasure seekers to enjoy the concerts, lovers' walks, fortune-tellers, sideshows, fireworks and dancing. A lake with landscaped gardens and rustic seats competed with fountains, birds in aviaries, and a small zoo devised to fit in with the rural surroundings. The bowling room, the ballroom and other places of interest were lit with gas manufactured in the gardens, and the popular fireworks displays included the Fortress of Sebastopol and the Mountain of Vesuvius. Here in the gardens was staged the first Australian ascent in a gas-filled balloon. Private and chartered houseboats crowded the river banks and many a champagne party was held on board a comfortably-appointed vessel while the guests threw pennies for which Aborigines dived into the Yarra.

The Yarra River had been given its name through a misunderstanding by J. H. Wedge of Batman's Port Phillip Association. The native name for the river was 'Birr-arrung', but when Wedge noticed boys pointing to the river and calling 'yarra yarra' he supposed this to be the real name. Later, when he heard Aborigines using the same word about another stream he realised that the word meant 'flowing flowing'. In the earliest days the river was spelt in many different ways, from 'Yarra Yarra' to 'Yarrow Yarrow' and 'Yarro Yarro', but although Wedge's mistake was well known, the name he had given was never changed except to be shortened to Yarra.

In the earliest days the pioneers drew their own water from the stream, but by 1839 a group of monopolists had erected pumps along the river banks, then leased them to water carriers who sold their loads at prices from three shillings to ten shillings a barrel of 120 gallons. There were many complaints that slaughter-yards and other noxious trades were polluting the water, and in 1840 speakers at public protest meetings contended that twenty people a week were dying of a mysterious disease called 'colonial fever' caused by the polluted water.

By the time this drawing was made, conditions had improved. Statutes had been passed forbidding pollution of the stream from fellmongeries, starch and glue factories, as well as boiling-down works. Richmond had become a municipality in 1855 and George Coppin who had done so much to publicise the district was appointed a councillor. Later in 1858 he was elected to the Legislative Council as representative of the South Western Province which included Richmond. He became a member of the Assembly in 1874 and continued till 1889. He is however, best remembered for his services to the theatre and for the extraordinary showmanship he brought to Cremorne Gardens at Richmond, where not the least of his delightful and enduring accomplishments was the acclimatisation of imported English thrushes and white swans. Their descendants can still be seen and heard in the Botanic Gardens.

Approach to Richmond, from North Bank of Yarra Yarra.

Published by Sands & Kenny, Melbourne & Sydney 1857

44   *The date of this drawing is not known but it is obviously later than 1854 because the trucks on the pier bear the inscription 'M. & H.B.R. Co.', standing for the Melbourne and Hobson's Bay Railway Company which had opened Australia's first railway between Melbourne and Sandridge (Port Melbourne) in 1854. Moreover the ships in the background, if studied through a magnifying glass, can well be said to 'present a forest of masts', a phrase commonly used by writers in Victoria in the 1850s when recording how ships' crews sometimes deserted almost in a body to try their luck on the goldfields. 'The Bay,' says one writer, 'was full of shipping from Williamstown to Sandridge, nothing but one complete forest of masts . . . between six and seven hundred ships were crowding each other for more room.' In fact, more than nine hundred ships arrived during 1853.*

Blackwood's Magazine claimed that the gold rush saved the British shipowner from ruin. Any ship that could stand the voyage from Europe was refitted and repainted to meet the demand for passages. On arrival in Melbourne, a ship's captain usually got his passengers off as soon as possible so that he might watch his crew. Many were prepared to desert ship in spite of the plain warning given by a large sign 'Refractory Seamen' painted on a white prison hulk in the bay. Crews often had already caught the wild excitement of passengers when the Victorian coastline was sighted. 'Men chased each other along the deck, shouted, leaped and seemed driven almost frantic', writes the level-headed Rev. Robert Young.

One of Melbourne's most unusual and delightful pioneers, Wilbraham Frederick Evelyn Liardet, is always associated with Sandridge (Port Melbourne), where he arrived in 1839 when the beach was 'clean and white and there was a great variety of lovely shells and thousands of wildflowers'. But he had no sooner arrived than he was off on business to Sydney, 600 miles away, leaving his wife and nine children to camp on the beach in tents lined with green baize. For company they had good neighbours in two fishermen named Adams and Story, who lived nearby in a large hogshead which had once contained sugar.

In later years Liardet and his family invited early settlers to seine fishing on moonlight nights when the intervals between catching fish were filled in with singing and accompaniments on the guitar. Liardet had established a ferry service and in 1840 he added a free mail service from the seaside to the city. He also opened the Brighton Pier Hotel, later the Pier Hotel, which became the centre of social life. Regattas on the Bay were planned; archery was introduced and taken up by Government House; the first family life-saving club was founded and saved, it is said, about forty lives; a special lifeboat was introduced; race meetings were organised.

Richard Howitt, one of Melbourne's prominent citizens, described Mrs Liardet as 'a tall, good-looking woman' who suddenly appeared out of the blackness with a bottle of wine and a wineglass to offer him a drink as he sat by his small fire on the beach. He was served with 'an especially fine port' before she chased off the children to light a beacon to guide back her husband returning from Williamstown, whither he had rowed a new arrival. Liardet planned to write a monumental history of Victoria but never finished it; however, he painted about forty delightful water-colours of early Melbourne which happily are preserved, with his notes, in the La Trobe Library at the State Library.

Sandridge, Williams Town, from Railway Pier.

Published by Sands & Kenny. Melbourne & Sydney. 1857

46 'The Yarra Yarra,' said pioneer J. H. Wedge who named the stream inaccurately, 'is a twisted cantankerous river . . . so choked with the trunks and branches of trees and other obstructions that it renders its navigation a matter of difficulty and delay to even the smallest of coasters.' Another writer, speaking of the same stretch of the river—which is shown in this engraving—was somewhat ecstatic: 'large trees like lines of foliaged sentinels guarded both sides and their branches protruded so far riverwise as to more than half shadow the stream. The waters were bright and sparkling; and, wooed by the fragrant acacias, shaking their golden blossom curls, the Yarra swarmed with a sort of black fish, bream, flounder and herring . . . the porpoises used to venture not only out of the bay but were sometimes rash enough to indulge in an aquatic stroll as far as Richmond . . . seals have been caught at a place now known as Fisherman's Bend.'

Until the fifties, some attempt had been made to keep the upper reaches of the Yarra clean so that at least that part of the river from which the drinking water of the city was drawn, above the falls at Queen Street, should be reasonably clean. Nevertheless, people complained that the garrison troops were using it as a regimental bath and several people were fined for bathing above the freshwater mark at Queen's Bridge. But below the falls, where the river was salt tidewater from the bay, no such restriction was insisted upon and the overgrown stream which had been an angler's delight far too quickly became 'a foetid, festering sewer . . . amidst the horrors of wool washing, fellmongering, bone crushing and other unmentionable abominations'.

It was inevitable that noxious trades requiring water should congregate on the river, but their growth was accelerated by the depression of the forties when sheep were worth practically nothing, when their meat was sold for one penny a pound, and when they were melted down for their fat. Often the hind legs were almost worthless because they held little fat, and they were sold for fourpence and fivepence apiece. Even this price attracted so few buyers that hundreds of legs were tipped into the river.

In the circumstances, when fumes and smoke and smells were giving to Melbourne the title of 'Beautiful Smellbourne' and gradually ruining the social reputation of the western end of the city, the successive great floods of 1842, 1844, 1848 and 1849 had their advantages. In 1844, the 'boiling-down establishments and slaughter-houses westward of the city were swept away.' In 1849, so much meat was lost in flooded slaughter-houses that there was talk of a meat famine. The river became a horrible mess of broken furniture, wood, old trees, pigs and poultry, as well as the remnants of 2,500 sheep which floods had overwhelmed at Philpot's boiling-down works. Despite these setbacks to slaughtering and associated activities, an official report of 1851 talks about the horrifying impurities in the water caused by abattoirs, starch and glue factories, tanneries and other noxious trades.

A year later, when hundreds of gold rush migrants invaded the city but could find no accommodation, they slept alongside the wharves in anything giving shelter, from old tanks to rusty boilers. To house some of them temporarily, the government took over some old abattoirs buildings at the foot of Batman's Hill—but men accommodated had to sweep and work for the town council between seven and nine o'clock in the morning.

A versifier, 'Juvenis', in April 1844 summed up the results of the concentration of slaughtering trades:

At Melbourne, some few months ago,
When stock was selling very low,
Our settlers hurried to and fro,
    And looked and talked despairingly.

And now on Yarra's bank a scene
Of fearful carnage may be seen,
And bloodier work than e'er has been
    At Linden, Prague or Waterloo.

Approach to Melbourne from Abattoir!

Published by Sands & Kenny, Melbourne & Sydney, 1857.

PRINCE'S BRIDGE & CITY TERMINUS OF M. & H. B. RAILWAY, MELBOURNE

The need for a bridge over the Yarra was recognised in the earliest days of the settlement, but not until 1845 was the first of three Princes Bridges built to give a more direct connection with ships anchored in the Bay. Until then, passengers and luggage were transferred to either flat-bottomed barges or boats which put them ashore at Williamstown, leaving them an uncomfortable nine-mile journey by horse or bullock dray to the settlement. Alternatively, passengers were loaded into small craft which took them about the same distance up the river. The quickest way was, of course, three miles overland from Port Melbourne, but only inadequate ferries were available at the river to take passengers across to the main settlement on the other side.

The first regular ferry was a row boat worked by Paddy Byrne and his daughter Polly. Horses and cattle had to be swum or walked across a reef or series of rapids close to the site of the present Princes Bridge. Henry Watts' ferry which followed was more elaborate and was launched with the traditional champagne and given the name Melbourne. It looked like two very big bullock drays lashed together. Passengers were charged twopence, a gig a shilling and a loaded dray two and sixpence. Later, a punt was introduced by a future mayor of Melbourne, John Hodgson. It was pulled backwards and forwards by a rope but, as a local of the day reported, 'it was still very unpleasant when the bullocks and passengers got mixed up'. A merry bricklayer, while giving an exhibition of walking on the punt rope fell into the river and was drowned. Matters looked more promising when the Melbourne Bridge Company's prospectus announced the building of 'an elegant and substantial suspension bridge at a cost of £4,500'. But the company merely took over a number of punts, made larger profits, 'doubled the toll on Sundays, but carried aldermen free'.

By 1845 the first bridge was across the Yarra. Seventeen feet wide and costing £530, it was quite inadequate, and in the following year the foundations of a much larger bridge were being laid. With a span of 150 feet, it was one of the longest in the world at that time, only two feet short of London Bridge. Governor La Trobe opened the bridge during the separation celebrations in November 1850.

In 1852 the Melbourne and Hobson's Bay Railway Company was formed with a capital of £100,000 to build a railway between the city and Port Melbourne. At the time the cost of horse and cart transport from Port Melbourne and Williamstown often doubled the price of goods landed there. Such transport cost between £2,000,000 to £3,000,000 a year, in addition to the costs of police protection.

In June 1853, the directors of the railway company had a trial run in an experimental train drawn by a 4-horsepower pile-driver lashed to one of the ballast trucks. Carriages and engines had been ordered from England for the projected opening but within ten weeks of the opening date only the carriages had arrived. The company therefore gave a contract for a locomotive to local engineers Robertson, Martin & Smith, and Langland's Port Phillip Foundry. On 12 September 1854, after having been presented with the Company's by-laws and timetable printed on silk, Governor Hotham and his party sat down in a first-class carriage upholstered in bright red plush and with brass oil lamps hanging from the ceiling. *The band of Her Majesty's 40th Regiment, seated in an open truck behind the engine, played the salute, and the train, cheered by thousands, started its triumphant ten-minute journey. At Port Melbourne it was welcomed by salutes from the warships* Electra *and* Fantome *and another hundred ships in the bay were gaily dressed for the occasion.*

Princes Bridge, & City Terminus of M. & H. B. Railway, Melbourne.

Published by Sands & Kenny, Melbourne & Sydney 1857.

QUEEN'S WHARF, MELBOURNE, WEST END

The position of Queen's Wharf, opposite what used to be the Customs House in Flinders Street (before it became the headquarters for Federal Members of Parliament visiting Melbourne) was determined by the limits to which salt water and ships could travel up the Yarra River. Across the river, immediately above what was Queen's Wharf, was a shelf of rock about a hundred feet wide, leaving only a small passage up which tiny boats could be dragged from the basin or pool of the river below. This was the point of which Batman wrote when he made in his diary the oft-quoted entry, '. . . about six miles up the river, all good water and very deep'.

In Melbourne's very early days, Surveyor Robert Hoddle proposed making a dam at this part of the river and suggested that the cost could be covered by the sale of land south of the river. He pointed out that when the tide fell four feet, only one foot of water flowed over the reef for one third of its length. It was agreed that a dam should be built, but floods in 1839 and again in 1842 swept away most of the work on it.

Queen's Wharf probably was so named by Governor Bourke in 1837 to honour Queen Victoria, who ascended the throne that year. Wharfage collected between June 1839 and October 1840, amounting to £2,561, was used to improve the so called 'wharf' which was in fact a courtesy title; vessels had to be tied to posts sunk a dozen or so yards out from the river bank.

Meantime Captain G. W. Cole, who had bought a waterside allotment nearby, built the first wooden wharf on the Yarra bank. He carved out a private anchorage from thick tea-tree. James Dobson, two years later in 1843, received permission to build a wharf alongside Col's Wharf, but La Trobe said that no further sales of waterside frontages would be made. An exception was made in 1853 for a private wharf for the P. and O. Line which had received the right to carry mails between England and Victoria. Meanwhile, the government pressed ahead with the building of Queen's Wharf, which became the most important wharf on this stretch of the river. The bridging of the river in 1930 at Spencer Street took away much of the wharf's importance.

In 1841 the Vesta *an iron ship which Manton Brothers had brought out in parts from England, was assembled near Queen's Wharf. She became a popular steamer, ferrying up and down the Yarra and taking racegoers to and from Flemington Racecourse via the Yarra and Maribyrnong Rivers. Another popular ship was the* Shamrock *which was the centre of attraction when it arrived in Melbourne on its monthly trip between Melbourne and Sydney. Other popular ships were the* City of Melbourne, *the first wooden steamer built on the Yarra, and the* Thames, *the first screw steamer to run between Melbourne and Geelong.*

Between 1877 and 1887, the watercourse of the Yarra was greatly improved. Sir John Coode, an eminent English engineer, had prepared plans to widen the river, and build docks as well as a canal to cut off a tortuous bend. Although some City councillors criticised his fee of £5,250, Sir John's plan of cutting a canal 2,000 feet long, 300 feet wide and 25 feet deep from near Queen's Wharf to Port Melbourne was adopted.

Queen's Wharf, Melbourne, West End.

Published by Sands & Kenny, Melbourne & Sydney, 1857.

THE UNIVERSITY OF MELBOURNE

Sir Redmond Barry, Judge of the Supreme Court of Victoria, was the first Chancellor of the University of Melbourne. On his death in 1880, the Council of the University paid its tribute to his long and valuable services in a resolution which ran: 'Its [the University's] initiation is attributable to his foresight and sagacity at a period of great wealth but intense excitement in suggesting to the Government the necessity for commencing an institution which at the time, by all minds but his, was regarded as premature and unnecessary.' This was not quite accurate. Although Barry was a great friend of the university, he cannot be given the exclusive, nor even the main, credit for its foundation. The real founder was a migrant, Hugh Culling Eardley Childers, later Chancellor of the Exchequer in Britain, whose original draft of the Bill to establish the university is now one of its most valued possessions.

Carrying a letter of introduction from a relative, Secretary of State for the Colonies Earl Grey, Childers, aged twenty-three, arrived in Melbourne in October 1850 and was shortly afterwards appointed Inspector of Schools at £250 a year. Two years later he had become Auditor-General at a salary of £1,200, with a seat in the nominated Legislative Council where, in his first speech on 4 November 1852, he proposed that £10,000 should be allotted to establish a university. 'After all,' he said, 'Sydney has a university and I would trust that before long Melbourne also would be able to boast of one.'

Several sites were suggested. An area near the present Parliament House was ruled out because it was too valuable; another south of the Yarra on the Domain Gardens was covered by a canvas town sheltering thousands of migrants who paid five shillings per tent, and the government was not willing to give up this revenue and face the task of finding an alternative site. So the present site of one hundred acres was set aside by the government, sixty acres reserved for colleges and forty for the university buildings.

Edward Bateman, an inexperienced landscape gardener who had planned the Carlton (Exhibition) Gardens, tackled the job of transforming rough and swampy land cut by a gully and covered by acres of rubbish and scarred by the many tracks of wheeled vehicles. He laid out terraces, avenues and roads, had thousands of tons of soil carted in, drained the water-sodden ground and added attractive trees, shrubs and lawns.

On 3 July 1854, Governor Sir Charles Hotham laid the foundation stone of the university so effectively that no one now knows where it is; the custom then was for an inscription to be engraved on a brass plate placed in a cavity covered with the next course of stones. The architect—chosen by a panel of judges on the basis of designs submitted by architects—was Francis Maloney White who won a prize of £300. He proposed a quadrangle with an ornamental front in Tudor style. In the finished building, five stone shields with armorial bearings were carved on the east and west walls. The north wing carried the arms of the building committee: the Chancellor Sir Redmond Barry, the Vice-Chancellor Hugh Childers, Lauchlan Mackinnon, W. F. Stawell and Francis Murphy. White's planned south wing, to complete the quadrangle, was never built because the government was short of money; this south wing would have had a square tower and a central archway.

This first building, with its cloisters, honey-coloured freestone and battlemented parapets, is now dwarfed by the massive buildings of the modern expanded University of Melbourne. The original building was first occupied in October 1855; there were four professors, and sixteen students had enrolled to take Arts, the only course then available. But only eleven students faced the examiners at the end of the year; the others had left the course. All of the eleven passed except one.

The University of Melbourne.

Published by Sands & Kenny Melbourne & Sydney. 1857.

ST. FRANCIS CATHEDRAL, MELBOURNE

Neither of the two cathedrals in Melbourne stand on the first grants of land made to their denominations. St James' Old Cathedral, now in King Street near Flagstaff Gardens, was granted the first Church of England site, and St Francis' monastery or church, was built on the first government land given to the Roman Catholics.

The attraction of St Francis' church to the historian is that, as shown by Gill's drawing, comparatively little seems to have changed since it was completed in 1845. With a little imagination anyone can picture the congregation arriving at the church which, in its earliest days, was regarded as being 'out in the bush'.

The census taken by Constable James Dwyer in October 1836—a year after the foundation of Melbourne—showed that of the population of 224, fourteen were Roman Catholics. At first they met at the home of a 'pious French carpenter', Peter Bodecin, in Collins Street, where the Olderfleet now stands. Later they collected £120 to build a small wooden hut but by 1839 they were appealing in the local newspapers for help to build a more suitable 'edifice' and were asking for contributions from 'protestant and Christian brethren. . .' as well as members of their own congregation. The first settlers of Melbourne helped each other in the building of their churches and, after the successful appeal for funds, the likeable Father Patrick Bonaventure Geoghegan, the first priest, wrote that 'our thanks are gratefully offered to esteemed individuals of other persuasions who have so generously aided us in erecting a place to worship God'. Father Geoghegan had celebrated Melbourne's first Mass on 19 May 1839 in the unroofed store of Hogue & Campbell, at the north-east corner of Elizabeth and Little Collins Streets.

On 4 October 1841 the foundation stone of St Francis' was laid but the following morning it was found that the stone had been moved and all the coins put down with it, worth only thirty shillings, had been stolen. This upset many people who saw it as reflecting on Melbourne's tolerance; probably all it meant was that a thief knew where to pick up thirty shillings.

The nave of the church was completed by May 1842 and on 23 October 1845 the first Mass in St Francis' was celebrated. Architect Samuel Jackson's design for the church was clean and simple, in the shape of a cross, with graceful pinnacles to relieve the single buttresses, and with the southern pediment surmounted by a stone cross.

The two gum trees shown in the engraving have long since disappeared. The furthest one on the right-hand side once held a church bell but it was cut down in 1877 and replaced with a simple cross. More than £700 was subscribed for a new set of bells from Murphy's foundry in Dublin; they arrived in 1853. The first Catholic bishop of Melbourne, James Alipius Goold, had planned a special tower but this was never built and in 1868 the bells went to the then new St Patrick's Cathedral. Finally in 1902, as the result of efforts by Father William Quilter, a new bell ordered from the same foundry was placed in a belfry on the east side of the church.

The old gum tree on the left-hand side, was cut down in the 1920s, but only after many protests and a compromise—that the wood should be used to make three episcopal chairs, all of which are now in St Patrick's Cathedral.

St Francis Cathedral, Melbourne.

Published by Sands & Kenny, Melbourne & Sydney, 1857.

DIGHT'S MILL, YARRA YARRA

Surprisingly few Melbourne people know of Dight's Falls on the Yarra or have visited this historic spot only a couple of miles from the centre of the city. Yet one has only to take a small loop that cuts away from the Yarra Boulevard to the left just beyond Johnston Street to be taken up to the hill shown here, which now overlooks busy industrial suburbs as well as the fine public golf course at Yarra Bend.

Dight's Falls was first seen by Europeans thirty-two years before either Batman or Fawkner decided to settle on the site of Melbourne. Early in 1803, Surveyor-General Charles Grimes, with a party including Dr McCallum, surgeon, James Meehan and young James Flemming, an agricultural expert, was sent by Governor King from Sydney, in the schooner Cumberland to Port Phillip Bay to report on a suitable site for a settlement. On 2 February they landed between what is now Port Melbourne and St Kilda; they walked overland, and discovered the Yarra. The following day, Lieutenant Charles Robbins, commander of the Cumberland, with Giles and Flemming and five sailors, rowed up the Maribyrnong River, a tributary of the Yarra, as far as Solomon's Ford, Keilor. On 4 February they rowed up the Yarra and, with McCallum, had their Sunday dinner on the site of Melbourne at what was to become known as Batman's Hill, near today's Spencer Street Station. Later that day their journey upstream was halted by what was afterwards called Dight's Falls. Lieutenant Robbins climbed the hill seen in the drawing and reported 'gentle rising hills clothed for ten to fifteen miles'.

Late in 1835, only a few months after the foundation of Melbourne, John Gardiner, Captain Hepburn and Joseph Hawdon, who had brought their cattle through hundreds of miles of unexplored country from north of the Murray River, drove them across the Yarra at this point. Gardiner settled on an area which has his name today, not far from Scotch College.

In Melbourne's early days the Yarra was a fine river for fish. There are many tales of great catches of bream and perch and of other excellent fishing at Dight's Falls. Wild game abounded and trappers and shooters made a good living out of bandicoots, wild cats and possums from the land which the Yarra Bend golf course now occupies.

John Dight, the flour miller whose name was to be given to the falls, arrived in 1839. Up to that time, flour had been brought from Tasmania at a cost of between £20 and £40 a ton, but occasionally the settlement ran short of flour and newspapers printed suggestions for substitutes for bread. One storekeeper suggested rice (had he cornered the rice supply?). Another proposed mixing bran boiled in water with liquor. Others, more practical, suggested growing their own wheat and grinding it with small steel handmills. Clearly, larger mills were needed.

John Dight and Peter Hurlstone, both millers, arrived in the same year and John chose the Dight's Falls site for its water power. By building his mill here, John attracted other firms and factories, and paved the way for the development and expansion of the Melbourne industrial suburbs of Collingwood and Fitzroy.

John Dight employed a Sydney millwright to erect the mill and cut a stone race to provide the water power. Then, unexpectedly, the river level dropped and Dight decided to supplement water power with steam. A steam mill he ordered from England was lost at sea. He ordered another but when it arrived a depression had hit the settlement and the mill was transferred to a company. Then came fire followed by rebuilding; floods up to thirty-six feet above normal level; and final destruction of the mill by another fire.

John went to live at Albury on the Murray River but his brother Charles, a member of Victoria's first Legislative Council, stayed on and until 1878 owned paddocks in Collingwood which included the site of Victoria Park Station.

Dight's Mill, Yarra Yarra.

Published by Sands & Kenny, Melbourne & Sydney, 1856.

58 *Where the old signal station used to stand in what are now the Flagstaff Gardens, Professor George Balthasar von Neumayer set up his observatory with magnetic, nautical and meteorological instruments worth £2,000 given to him by the king of Bavaria. Neumayer had returned in 1852 to Bavaria, where he was born. He had had no success as a gold miner in Victoria but he was convinced that a valuable field of scientific research existed here.*

With the encouragement of his king and of a number of British scientists, he asked the Victorian Government to let him set up his observatory in the Domain; when this was refused he accepted the suggested alternative at the Flagstaff Hill signal station, which by then was outliving its usefulness. There he carried out research into atmospheric electricity and changes in magnetic elements; he wrote several valuable books and returned in 1863 to Germany where he was appointed to the Oceanic Observatory in Hamburg.

The history of Flagstaff Hill began in Melbourne's earliest days when a small cemetery was begun there. On 30 June 1836, less than a year after the start of the settlement, William, the small son of John and Mary Goodman, was the first white child to be buried. Within a fortnight, Charles Franks and his shepherd, killed by Aborigines in the country, were given graves here. Three others were buried in the tiny graveyard before an area was set aside for the first public cemetery where the Victoria Market was later built. They were an unnamed seaman from H.M.S. Rattlesnake, which had brought Captain Lonsdale to the settlement; the infant son of Mr and Mrs Wills, and the wife of John Ross.

After this funereal beginning, Flagstaff Hill became a gayer and livelier place. In 1840 it was decided to set up a signal station on the hill, which was already popular as a lookout for vessels coming up Hobson's Bay. Late in 1840, a mast to carry signalling flags was erected alongside a small octagonal building with dormer windows, inside which were to be found in 'the neatest possible array' telescopes and a full range of flags to indicate any type of ship entering the port. A year later the flagstaff was replaced by another pole some fifty feet high; a small cannon also placed on the hill was fired when important ships came into view. This signal often made shopkeepers put up their shutters while they hurried to Sandridge (Port Melbourne) to get the latest news from home.

In the 1840s, Flagstaff Hill was in the fashionable end of town. People picnicked here to read the latest shipping notices, listen to the 40th Regimental Band or use their telescopes to try to identify ships coming up the Bay. On 11 November 1850 a huge bonfire on the hill started a chain of bonfires on other hilltops to celebrate the news of Victoria's separation from New South Wales. One hundred years later, the then Governor of Victoria, Sir Dallas Brookes, unveiled a memorial which recalls the history and purpose of the flagstaff signal station.

One day during the Crimean War there was heavy firing in the Bay and the sentry at Flagstaff Hill announced that the Russians had arrived. Hundreds of men collected weapons, from pitchforks to guns, and raced to Port Melbourne. There they learned that the Great Britain, in quarantine till that night, had fired a salvo for joy when released. Other ships had joined in.

During the gold rush word went round that gold had been found on Flagstaff Hill. It was a hoax; somebody had scattered shining brass filings on the grass.

Hobson's Bay, &c. from Signal Station.

in Sands & Kenny, Melbourne & Sydney 1857.

60 The National Model and Training School, Melbourne, built on an irregularly-shaped piece of ground of about two and a half acres bounded by Albert, Spring, Victoria and Evelyn Streets, was opened on 18 September 1854 to improve educational methods and to 'show Sydney something of the conception of a model school with model teachers and model scholars'. The grant of land, originally intended for a market, was made to the Board of National Education on a 'quit rent of one peppercorn yearly for ever on demand'.

This national board had been set up in 1852 to organise and build non-denominational or State schools at a total cost of £25,000. A Denominational School Board had been created four years earlier to control church schools that were receiving, by 1852, about £20,000 a year in grants of aid. The original idea had been that all schools should be controlled by one authority, but the churches were too jealous of their privileges.

The Model School cost £45,000 before it was opened. The handsome building had a chiming turret clock above a coat-of-arms which surmounted the doorway. The salary of the first teachers, Mr and Mrs Arthur Davitt, specially brought from Ireland, was good for its day, although the £1,000 a year they were jointly paid was well earned. In less than three months 705 pupils were 'scribbling with pencils and paper from Ireland'.

The school incorporated many revolutionary ideas and was co-educational, but all boys entered by the Victoria Street entrance, while the girls used the Evelyn Street gate—the Albert Street entrance was used by the school council. Moreover, the girls and boys, although educated together, always played separately with a hardwood fence dividing the two play-yards. This offered a challenge to the more daring pupils. One of them—later a famous actress, Nellie Stewart—regularly raided the ring where the boys played 'knuckledown'. Pupils' fees ranged from a shilling to four shillings a week paid ten weeks in advance. Parents and friends were welcome to inspect the school.

In 1862, the school's name was changed to Central Common School and in 1868 the first university scholarship was won by a pupil, Frank Goldstraw, later headmaster of Wesley College. In 1872, the newly formed Department of Education had its offices at the school but these were moved in 1878. By 1890 the school had become simply State School No. 391, but in 1905 it was revived as the Melbourne Continuation School, the first of many schools instituted under the new system of State secondary education. The school gradually won a fine reputation under its headmaster, Mr J. Hocking, and headmistress, Miss Margery Robertson. Although it had another change of name in 1912 to the Melbourne High School, it continued as a co-educational school.

In the late 1920s, all the boys were moved to a new building on Forrest Hill, South Yarra—the Melbourne Boys' High School. The deserted girls remained at the old school in Spring Street for a few years later and then moved to the stately surroundings of State Government House. One more move to King Street, and then the girls settled down in MacRobertson Girls' High School, the gift of Sir Macpherson MacRobertson, the wealthy chocolate manufacturer. On 9 October 1934, the Duke of Gloucester opened this school, adding that he hoped the young ladies would be pleased with it 'although the space allotted for dancing is not quite as large as the ballroom at Government House'.

National Model & Training School, Melbourne.

Published by Sands & Kenny, Melbourne & Sydney. 1857.

62 On 13 December 1842 Melbourne's first four aldermen, eight councillors and Henry Condell, mayor of the newly-incorporated town, dressed for a procession through the streets. They had designed their own uniform of which a blue cloth coat with wide swallow tails was part; it was lined with white satin and embroidered with the letters VR in gilt. Each man wore a shiny bell topper and beautifully polished high-heeled Wellington boots. After the procession they were sworn in at the Court House by the irascible Judge Willis, who treated them to corned-beef sandwiches and sherry and water.

Melbourne had become a Town, but it had to wait fourteen years for its first Town Hall. The site was the excuse for many bitter quarrels. Some people suggested that part of the land belonging to St James' Church of England at the corner of Collins and William Streets should be made available because this was the fashionable end of town. Others suggested fifteen acres where Parliament House is now. Finally the present site at the corner of Collins and Swanston Streets—described as a 'narrow slip of land in a dusty, noisy thoroughfare'—was conveyed to the City Council. By this time (June 1894) Melbourne had become a city. The Town Hall was completed in 1854 although the disappearance of artisans for the gold fields had threatened to delay it indefinitely.

Before it was finished it had caused some excitement in London. A Government House was being planned at the same time and a sketch of 'a huge, elegant but cherished piece of proposed extravagance . . . costing £200,000' had been prepared. This was reproduced in the London Illustrated papers and described as the Melbourne Town Hall, which was in fact a heavy bluestone building 'doubtfully relieved with dingy granite'. This Town Hall lasted only thirteen years. The city fathers wanted a grander, bigger building for a city growing in importance and which was about to welcome its first Royal visitor, the Duke of Edinburgh, who laid the foundation stone of the new building on 29 November 1867.

The old Police Court and station which had been built between 1847 and 1849 stood by the side of the new Town Hall for many years. For years, too, cabs worked from a stand opposite the Town Hall although, says one embittered overseas visitor, 'only diggers and the labouring classes could afford these conveyances . . . which crowd the streets to the suburbs in numbers not met with in England outside London'.

A year after this engraving was printed, an arcaded front was added to the small courtyard and low balustraded wall in front of the Court, which brought it up to the building line in Swanston Street. The Court stood there for another thirty years until 1888, when the Council bought the site from the government for £140,000. But the frontage was converted into shops when the collapse of the land boom made previous plans for new council buildings impracticable. Another twenty years passed before a new administrative block replaced the temporary shops. The square tower contained a bell that summoned the local fire brigade which, in the flowery words of a contemporary writer, 'by means of the now plentiful supply of water from the Yan Yean, soon has the mastery of the devouring elements'.

Perhaps the most lasting reminder of the first Town Council is the present official seal of Melbourne which was designed for it by a fine engraver, and member of a well-known Melbourne family, Mr John Ham, in August 1842. It shows a golden fleece for wool, a whale for oil, a bull for tallow, and a sailing ship for exports, in a quartering symbolic of the young settlement's trade. The inscription 'We gather strength as we go' from Virgil's Aeneid was certainly honoured in the great days of the gold rush.

City Police Station and Town Hall, Melbourne.

Published by Sands & Kenny, Melbourne & Sydney, 1857.

POST OFFICE, MELBOURNE

64 *Apart from the Victorian gold miner's longing to make a rich strike, nothing exceeded his longing for news from home. One of the sights of Melbourne in the 1850s was hundreds of diggers queueing at this Post Office for a letter. Standing by, with impatient drivers ready to dash off to country centres, stood Cobb & Co. coaches. By the mid-fifties, when mail was being sent regularly overseas, small booths had been erected and stamps, paper and even the services of a letter writer were available. By that time, too, post offices had been established in the country, and a four-horse carriage was carrying mails between Melbourne and Sydney where previously the mail link had been sustained by a solitary mailman on horseback, who knew what it was to swim swollen streams, face danger from marauding Aborigines and be held up by bushrangers.*

The Post Office was established in 1841 at the corner of Elizabeth and Bourke Streets. It rapidly became the centre of community life, and there was some excitement when fights broke out over the 'right time'. Even the town's watchmakers could not agree. A subscription was taken up for a public clock but when it arrived, no one could agree where it should be set up. Some suggested a nearby gum tree; ultimately the clock had to wait until a small clock-tower was added to the Post Office; even there, it continued to confound everyone by being either an hour fast or an hour slow.

In earlier years letters were at first left at John Batman's house, and later several unofficial post offices were used. The first official postmaster was Captain Benjamin Baxter, Clerk of the Bench. His wife carried out nearly all the postal duties until that day in March 1839 when the Yarra flooded her small post office in a cottage near the corner of King Street and Flinders Lane and she and her children were rescued by boat. The cold that resulted was so severe that Captain Baxter gave up his £150 a year position.

David Kelsh was postmaster when the Post Office was moved from Chancery Lane to the Elizabeth and Bourke Streets corner. The title to the land gives the postal authorities the right to sink wells for 'domestic, farming, agricultural or irrigation purposes'. Sometimes irrigation seemed to be the last thing this area needed, for in those early days Elizabeth Street often became a dangerously flooded gully in wet weather. Perversely, in the summer, slow-moving bullock teams transformed it into a dust bowl. The soggy ground made building slow when the new Post Office was being built. In eight years, only the first two storeys had been erected. When the third storey was finally added, today's more reliable clock was supplied. With its twelve bells, it plays twenty-eight different tunes, seven hymns and twenty-one old songs.

In the middle forties, two pillar boxes had been placed at either end of the town, from which a gorgeously dressed letter carrier in scarlet coat and gold-laced hat collected the mail. Later, gaily-dressed telegraph messengers set out on horseback from the Post Office, a brass band in bright uniform played on the steps, and departmental heads arrived at work in shining silk toppers and frock coats. From these early days the Post Office has remained one of the popular city centres. Many old-timers still settle down on warm sunny days to talk and smoke on the broad bluestone steps that face Elizabeth Street. It is still Melbourne's rendezvous for New Year celebrations.

S T Gill, del.   J Tingle s

Post Office, Melbourne.

Published by Sands & Kenny, Melbourne & Sydney, 1857

ST. PAUL'S CHURCH FROM SOUTH END OF SWANSTON STREET, MELBOURNE

66 The St Paul's Church shown here stood on the present site of St Paul's Cathedral at the corner of Flinders and Swanston Streets. In the first year of the settlement Dr Alexander Thompson, medical officer of the Port Phillip Association and catechist, held weekly Church of England services in a tent nestling under a great gum tree at this corner. It was originally intended to build a court house here but in late 1841, the area was leased to a contractor as a hay and corn market. In return for the profits of the business he undertook to provide a shed, and weighbridge, as well as act as inspector. But, in 1847, when the Eastern market was established in Bourke Street, he moved his business to what he considered was a more promising site.

The vacant allotment was Bishop Charles Perry's opportunity. He had been looking for a better site for the Church of England, whose St James' Church was situated in what was slowly becoming the less central and desirable part of the city—at the corner of William and Little Collins Streets. In reply to his request Surveyor Robert Hoddle wrote on 8 March 1848 that he 'saw no objection . . . to the use of this site . . . as it is not now required for the purpose originally intended . . . or for a gaol and courthouse which are built in another part of the city'.

The foundation stone of the new church, intended to be the parish Church of St Paul's, was laid in 1850. A handsome bluestone building, it had accommodation for 2,000 people who crowded in to hear the opening service by Dean Macartney, who later preached the last sermon when the church made way for St Paul's Cathedral. The foundation stone of the Cathedral was laid in 1880 by the Marquis of Normanby, the Governor of Victoria, and the new Cathedral was consecrated in 1891.

St Paul's Church was the work of Bishop Perry; St Paul's Cathedral was his dream, but his appeal for money was unsuccessful and it required the energy and organising ability of his successor, Bishop Moorhouse, to overcome the many difficulties.

Perry, compared with that 'mountain of a man' Moorhouse, looked a bookish man but he had tremendous energy, visiting the length and breadth of his diocese, often travelling fifty and sixty miles to preach at gold towns and diggings three times in the one day. At Forest Creek the 'congregation consisted of about two hundred people morning and evening', writes Mrs Perry, 'and about four hundred in the afternoon. They behaved with perfect propriety during the service . . . C [Charles] was compelled to perform the afternoon service in his riding dress, and his pulpit being the stump of a tree, which afforded rather a precarious footing, you may imagine that he did not present a very clerical appearance.' Perry spent two months on the goldfields and had some dangerous experiences there. Once he was distributing tracts at a goldfields settlement, when 'the horse stumbled and fell, throwing him forward on his face and actually rolling on his back . . . fortunately the dust was very deep . . . and furnished a soft bed for him to fall on . . . C [Charles] says it was a most remarkable escape.'

Although disappointed that he did not see the building of St Paul's Cathedral, Perry felt that the foundation of Trinity College, one of the residential colleges at the University of Melbourne, and his success in dividing his huge diocese into two by founding that of Ballarat was more important. When he resigned in 1876, he was made a Prelate of the Order of St Michael and St George. He was for some time Canon of Llandaff Cathedral in Wales; he died at the age of 84, in 1891, the year that his dream came true—when St Paul's Cathedral was consecrated.

St. Paul's Church from South End of Swanston St. Melbourne.

Published by Sands & Kenny, Melbourne & Sydney, 1857.

GT. COLLINS ST. LOOKING EAST FROM WESLEYAN CHAPEL, MELBOURNE

Collins Street has always been one of Melbourne's important streets. Until about the time this drawing was made, the western end was the more fashionable and influential. A block beyond this point, at the corner of William Street, the first land in the city was auctioned in 1837; John Batman built a two-storey building there and in 1839 the commission of Superintendent Charles La Trobe was read there. On the opposite side of the street was the first Church of England reserve where a small building served several denominations. Between William and Queen Streets stood the famous Lamb Inn where several of the first clubs were founded and where, on 2 January 1838, John Conway Bourke set off with the first overland mail to Sydney. Opposite was the first gaol and the stocks used to punish drunks.

At this corner, Queen Street, the Union Bank shown in the drawing stands on the site of Melbourne's first bank, the Derwent Banking Company, which opened its hopeful doors to a small public on 8 February 1838. On the other corner to the left stood several interesting hotels, the first of which was the Angel Inn; the licence, one of the first in the city, was held by Edward Umphelby, who bought the allotment in the first sales for £61.

Down from this corner, on the left-hand side and on the present site of the Commonwealth Bank, stood the Imperial Hotel, later the Grand Imperial where the dancer Lola Montez stayed. Another equally well-known hotel was the Royal, on the site opposite the A.N.Z. Bank; at the Royal the first councillors and aldermen met to appoint their mayor, Henry Condell, staunch Presbyterian and brewer, who later led the official procession up Collins Street in a flapping scarlet cloak which caused panic and confusion among the bullock teams, and probably provoked the bullock drivers to lurid eloquence. In May of that same year, 1842, one hundred and twenty Gentlemen Volunteers celebrated the capture of three bushrangers. By the 1890s everyone who was anyone had to be seen at midday on the Block, between Elizabeth and Swanston Streets. Fortunately cartoonist Phil May was also often there and he left a treasury of drawings of actors, politicians, artists and beautiful women. The fashionable place to eat was Gunsler's Vienna Cafe, on the site of the Hotel Australia.

Several factors contributed to the early importance of Melbourne's western end. The town was split in two by Elizabeth Street which, in rainy weather, became a roaring torrent. All the early official buildings were near Queen's Wharf. Another early disadvantage for the eastern end was the very steep slope of Collins Street from Swanston Street to Russell Street. Both the Presbyterian and Independent congregations complained bitterly that the sites for their churches at the corners of Collins and Russell Streets made them 'too far out of town'. In 1849, after many protests, thousands of tons of rock were blasted out to make the slope easier; after that Collins Street began to expand eastwards. Even then, said one writer, the slope remained 'a precipice down which Her Majesty's subjects are at liberty to break their necks . . . the only benefit that is likely to arise is the appointment of a coroner'.

So neglected was the eastern part of Collins Street in early days that on 17 August 1840 blocks of land were advertised for auction 'for those of the labouring class who require a residence in town for the purpose of having their children near school and of being close to shops where they could procure their working implements'.

Ironically, Collins Street is named after Captain David Collins whose wholehearted condemnation in 1803 of the Port Phillip area as a place for settlement did so much to delay the foundation of Melbourne.

Gt. Collins St. looking East, from Wesleyan Chapel, Melbourne.

VICTORIA ILLUSTRATED

SECOND SERIES

View of Point Gellibrand and Williamstown from Bay.

PUBLISHED BY SANDS, KENNY & Cº MELBOURNE, AND SANDS & KENNY, SYDNEY.

1862

NICHOLAS CHEVALIER

It is doubtful whether Nicholas Chevalier was the author of all the drawings in the 1862 edition of Victoria Illustrated, but it can be said that they were not the work of S. T. Gill, who was credited with them by William Moore in his Story of Australian Art and by later commentators who followed Moore's error. The frontispiece—'View of Point Gellibrand and Williamstown from the Bay'—is shown as drawn by Chevalier and engraved by A. Willmore. The forty engravings in the book, however, have only Willmore's name as engraver and, although it is agreed that Chevalier contributed substantially to the 1862 edition, the experts have been unable to designate his work with precision. The account books of the Melbourne publishers, Sands and Kenny, would have helped by showing who had been paid for the drawings, but these records have been destroyed. For the same reason, we do not know what Gill was paid for his forty-four drawings in the 1857 edition.

Chevalier's engravings chosen from the 1862 edition differ substantially from those of S. T. Gill; they concentrate on the material prosperity brought about by the previous ten golden years and reflected in the many splendid public and private buildings erected during that time. This would be natural, for Chevalier had little practical experience of the pioneering days of the Victorian gold rush. He did not arrive until 1855. Some said he came to look after the Australian investments of his father; others that he merely travelled out to join his brother on the goldfields. Whatever the reason, he stayed a very short time at the diggings where he and his brother had little luck.

Chevalier's father came from Vaud, Switzerland, but later held an important post in Russia, not in the Czar's household staff as some writers have suggested, but as an overseer on the estates of a Russian nobleman, Prince de Wittgenstein. He married a Russian girl who, on 9 May 1828 in St Petersburg, became the mother of Nicholas Chevalier.

Nicholas had a broader education than most youngsters of his age and class. He left Russia with his father in 1845 and travelled extensively in Europe. He studied lithography under Louis Gruner in London and illustrated in this medium. He also studied art in Rome, and architecture and painting in Munich. This interest in architecture is seen in his choice of drawings for the 1862 edition of Victoria Illustrated which is, in the main, concerned with buildings rather than people and places.

When he arrived in Melbourne in February 1855, he already had some small reputation as a water-colourist, having exhibited at the Royal Academy in London. Certainly he was soon attracting so many private commissions that he was forced to employ an assistant, young E. Wake Cook, who later became a well-known landscape painter in England. Cook was instructed in painting, wood engraving and lithography. Writing about his early experiences, he said that, in 1852, Melbourne suffered from an 'almost complete lack of the visual arts'. A few years later he was attracted to a painting in Wilkie's Melbourne music shop. It was William Strutt's Troopers, Mounted Police. Other paintings that he remembered in the same window were Ferntree Gully by Eugene von Guerard, and a view of the Yarra River by Nicholas Chevalier. He also mentions his excitement at seeing a collection of about fifty Gills hung in the vestibule of the Theatre Royal in Bourke Street.

The visual arts were given a helping hand when, on 2 August 1855, the first number of a periodical that was to become famous in Australia—Melbourne Punch—was issued. The first drawings were by a 'Mr Gill', no relation to S. T. Gill, but before the second number had appeared Chevalier had been appointed its first cartoonist. His successors, much later, included Hugh McCrae, Hal Gye who illustrated the first edition of C. J. Dennis' Sentimental Bloke and Percy Leason.

On 10 October 1856 the Victorian Society of Fine Arts was founded with a committee which included John Pascoe Fawkner, Charles Summers the sculptor, and painters William Strutt, Ludwig Becker and Nicholas Chevalier. The society held only one exhibition—in the old Exhibition Building on the present site of what was formerly the Royal Mint in William Street. Among the artists represented was Nicholas Chevalier.

After his resignation from Melbourne Punch in 1861, Chevalier travelled through Victoria making sketches, often in the company of the gifted Professor George Balthasar von Neumayer, hydrographer and meteorologist. The professor had come to Victoria under the patronage of the King of Bavaria to continue his scientific studies which were later to provide the material for his Results of the Magnetic Survey of the Colony of Victoria—1858-1864. In 1866, Chevalier was in New Zealand where he was voted £200 by its Provincial Council to assist him in his 'artistic labours'. In the edition of Notes and Queries which contains this information—2 June 1866—we are told that Chevalier had been awarded £250 by the Victorian Fine Arts Commission. The amount was, in fact, £200.

The Victorian Government under Sir James McCullock had appointed, in 1863, a Commission on Fine Arts to enquire into the promotion of local works of art. Its recommendations ultimately led to the establishment of the first public art gallery in Australia, in Melbourne on 24 December 1864, with £2,000 as the nucleus of a fund to buy works of art. In addition, a prize of £200 was offered for the best picture by an artist in Australia and it was from the forty-three submitted, that Nicholas Chevalier's Buffalo Ranges of Victoria was chosen. This picture, still in the National Gallery of Victoria, was purchased by the trustees and was the first Australian work to be acquired.

By the time the Duke of Edinburgh visited Melbourne in November 1867, Chevalier was back again in Australia—this time with the Australian Illustrated News. As its representative, he travelled around Victoria with the Royal party and so impressed the Duke with his abilities as an artist and musician that he was invited to join the Royal entourage on its return trip to London through the East. Meantime, a number of Chevalier's New Zealand paintings had been hung in the 1868 Paris Exposition, where they had been given favourable notices. After Chevalier's death in 1902, his widow gave a number of them to the government of New Zealand.

On his arrival in England with the Duke of Edinburgh, Chevalier busied himself organising a very successful exhibition in South Kensington of the 130 water-colours he had completed on the Royal Tour. He received many royal commissions, including a series of historical records of outstanding events in Queen Victoria's reign. In 1874, the Queen personally commissioned him to paint the wedding of the Duke of Edinburgh at St Petersburg—the city where Chevalier's father had arranged for his first drawing *lessons. Two of his more unusual royal commissions were drawings for the mounting of the Koh-i-nor diamond in the diadem of Queen Victoria, and a design for a fountain in the grounds of Osborne House, the royal residence on the Isle of Wight.*

Chevalier also maintained his interest in music. He belonged to the Royal Amateur Orchestral Society founded by members of H.M.S. Galatea, the ship on which the Duke of Edinburgh had travelled around the world. The Duke was a regular and proficient member of the first violins; Nicholas played with the seconds.

In London Chevalier's future was assured, He had an elegant house in Porchester Terrace, Hyde Park; for some twenty years after 1870 his works were hung annually at the Royal Academy: he mixed with the well-to-do and influential society of the day. By 1895, however, his health was failing and he had only one picture in that year's Royal Academy. He died seven years later on 15 March 1902. The Times obituary of 18 March stated that 'for twenty-three years he was honorary purchaser for the National Gallery of New South Wales, which is acknowledged to be the finest in Australasia'. Some might dispute that assessment but there is no doubt that Chevalier was a versatile and well-educated man who spoke several languages fluently, was a competent painter and musician, understood architecture and introduced chromo-lithography to Australia. He was survived by his wife, Caroline Wilkie, a relative of Sir David Wilkie, whom he had married in 1855 and who wrote his biography, Nicholas Chevalier Peintre Vaudois.

Chevalier was not a great Australian painter or artist. He broke no new ground as did Louis Buvelot, also of Swiss parentage. But he made a very real contribution to art and painting in Australia by his enthusiasm and industry in interesting the public in Australian subjects, in galleries, in exhibitions and in painting generally.

LIST OF ILLUSTRATIONS

Second Series

BANK OF NEW SOUTH WALES, MELBOURNE

76 The handsome structure erected by this Banking Company occupies one of the best sites in the city, being in Collins Street West, and was designed by Mr Reed. The Bank of New South Wales is the oldest monetary institution in Australia, having been established in Sydney as far back as the year 1817. The amount of its capital stock paid up is £750,000; its reserve fund £212,500. The rate of dividend last declared to the shareholders was 15 per cent per annum. Its gross liabilities in Victoria on the 31st March last, were £1,324,296 15s. 4d.; and its assets £1,840,458 15s. 8d. Its circulation of notes in the Colonies is £236,478 11s. 8d. It has numerous branches in New South Wales, Victoria, and New Zealand.

The facade of this building was copied from the Library of St Mark, Venice, one of the most beautiful works of the later Venetian renaissance. The library was designed by San Sovino in 1536 when he was one of the great architects of Venice, it became renowned for the delicacy of its carvings. The Bank of New South Wales, Melbourne, was not the only building that copied this superb facade; the Carlton Club, London, is one of many others.

The design was faithfully executed, not only by architect and workmen, but in particular by the sculptor Charles Summers who had returned unsuccessful from the goldfields to work on Parliament House, where the figures in the Council Chamber are his work. Summers later sculpted the impressive Burke and Wills memorial, with its beautifully wrought reliefs around the pedestal. The lovely carved spandrels, caps and friezes of the Bank of New South Wales facade are his work.

But while the bank's exterior was highly satisfying, the interior gave the directors anxious moments. The land where the bank stood (now occupied by the Commonwealth Bank between Queen and Elizabeth Streets in Collins Street) was bought for £6,000 in 1852. The architects were Messrs Reed & Barnes, and the builder Mr William Crocker Cornish, whose tender for 'the new banking house' was £23,779. By the time the bank opened (on 1 July 1858) it had cost just over £37,000, and the Melbourne manager was complaining that the architect had not properly superintended the work and that he had agreed to unauthorised expenses in decoration which had raised the cost far beyond the original estimate. The board of the bank ordered that the architect's commission be delayed.

Two years later the Melbourne manager was complaining that 'from the crushed state of the timber beams upon which the private apartments of the Bank rested, serious apprehension existed that that portion of the building would fall'. The board then directed that, although the architect's suggested repairs be carried out, the bank's solicitor should advise whether action should be taken against Reed for damages 'caused by his negligence and want of skill'. Two months later, in February 1861, the board was informed that the business of the bank would have to be transferred while the alterations were made, though these must 'be gone on with night and day so that the Bank might not be too long saddled with exorbitant rent'.

Despite these early fears, the building lasted until 1933 when the facade, including the carved stones signed 'Charles Summers 1858', was given to the new School of Commerce at the University of Melbourne. When the bank added a sizeable donation towards the new building it was expected that the school would be in a style of architecture suited to the fine facade. However, the elaborate Italianate front was merely stuck on to the rear of what was considered, in the thirties, to be a 'modern' building. It still clings there as an architectural orphan—a handsome, forlorn and rather ridiculous blank back wall.

Bank of New South Wales, Melbourne.

Sands, Kenny & Cº Melbourne   Sands & Kenny, Sydney

ORIENTAL BANK, MELBOURNE

78 Established in Melbourne in 1853. This Bank has a capital of £1,260,000, and a reserve fund of £252,000. The value of the notes in circulation, according to the latest official returns, was £238,216 10s., and the rate of dividend 14 per cent per annum. The liabilities in the colony on the average of the quarter ending 31st March, 1861, were £1,019,969 7s. 3d., and its assets £1,283,442 15s. 4d. No banking institution in Australia has probably such extensive ramifications as this.

In 1862, when this engraving was made, a number of banks had already capitalised on the extraordinary prosperity of the gold years. The Oriental had been in the vanguard. Originally it had occupied a 'rather stark red brick building' at 26 Queen Street but later it had moved to 'a magnificent white building, more like a Grecian temple' at 11-13 Queen Street. The original building had been leased to the National Bank of Australasia whose funds had, at one time during the directors' fight with the shareholders and founder Alexander Gibb, been locked up in this branch of the Oriental Bank.

A few years later, the Oriental had the unenviable responsibility of reporting to the same bank—the National—that its assets in the overseas branch at Mauritius were worthless. The National Bank had opened a branch there because of the considerable exchange business represented by the export of sugar from the island to Australia. Edward Mellish the manager had gone far beyond his authority in authorising credit as well as 'borrowing' funds for his own use. When the National Bank decided to ask the Oriental to realise all assets, it was too late. Another interesting link between the two banks was the cheque which the Kelly gang 'borrowed' from a homestead near Euroa and used as an excuse to enter and then hold up the local National Bank. This was drawn for 24s. on the Oriental Bank in Melbourne. The date was 9 December 1878.

Six years later, in May 1884, the once powerful Oriental Bank suspended payment in Australia. It had been, until then, one of London's largest overseas banks and had ruled its vast colonial banking empire from magnificent offices in Threadneedle Street, close to the Bank of England. Its collapse was partly due to its over-optimistic advances against sugar in Mauritius and coffee in Ceylon. However, it ultimately paid all its Australian depositors in full when a New Oriental Banking Corporation took over its remaining business.

But by this time Australian banks had grabbed, quite unceremoniously, most of the business of its twenty-two branches. Its old friend the National Bank had taken over its business at Castlemaine, Newstead, Dimboola, Nhill and Sydney, as well as some of its buildings and even two managers—at Castlemaine and Sydney. It was about this time that the National's chief manager said how much he deplored the takeover tendencies of the Bank of Australasia, which was writing to Oriental customers suggesting that they should change to the Australasia.

Oriental Bank, Melbourne.

Sands, Kenny & Co. Melbourne   Sands & Kenny, Sydney.

UNION BANK OF AUSTRALIA, MELBOURNE

This Banking Company was established in 1837, with a paid-up capital of £1,000,000, and a reserve fund of £213,540 5s. 4d. Having no charter its liability is unlimited. It has notes in circulation to the amount of £218,255 2s. 2d. Its aggregate liabilities on the 31st March, 1861, were £1,264,203 15s. 6d., and assets on same date £1,755,021 17s. 9d.; its last declared dividend was at the rate of 12 per cent per annum.

Even if all the facts were known—and they are not—it would be difficult to determine who founded the Union Bank; George Fife Angas or Philip Oakden. What is known is that a small colonial bank, the Tamar, opened in Launceston in January 1835, and that one of the founders was Philip Oakden. A year later the competition from the powerful Bank of Australasia, which had also established a Launceston branch, was so fierce that the directors agreed that Oakden should go abroad to negotiate with a group of Liverpool business men who were planning a United Banking Company of Australia to take over the Tamar Bank.

When the planners grew nervous about the project, Oakden decided to enlist the help of Angas whose name was a powerful and respected one in British banking and finance circles. Angas had, with his cousin Thomas Joplin, founded what is now one of the great British banks, the National Provincial. He had also played a big part in founding the Bank of South Australia. Angas became interested in Oakden's proposal and in his diary for May 1837, he recalls a discussion with Oakden as they walked across Southwark Bridge in London. After careful consideration, Angas agreed to meet the earlier promoters of the United Bank, and later, to lend his name to the project. Shrewdly, he insisted that if he did help to promote the new bank, it must not open branches in South Australia in opposition to his bank there.

On 6 July 1837, at a directors' meeting at which the Union Bank was virtually founded, decisions were made about the prospectus which was to be issued on the 1 September, 1837. This was never really needed, for Angas' name was so highly thought of that £250,000 in £25 shares was taken up immediately in London, while little difficulty was experienced in selling the remaining £250,000 worth of shares allocated to Australia.

Oakden was soon on his way home to Tasmania with 25,000 Mexican dollars and £20,000 in British coin. By 1 May 1838, the Tamar Bank had disappeared. The Union Bank opened in Melbourne in the following October. A month later the Melbourne branch of the Derwent Bank, whose head office was in Hobart, was taken over and its premises, shown here at the south east corner of Queen and Collins Streets, were occupied by the Union Bank. The first Melbourne manager, Mr W. F. A. Rucker, had been manager of the Derwent Bank which was run by Charles Swanston, a member of John Batman's Port Phillip Association who gave his name to one of Melbourne's best-known streets. The Union became a powerful organisation. It introduced banking to New Zealand with the first settlers and was one of the few banks which never closed its doors, even in the depression days of the 1890s.

However, its ancestor the Tamar Bank is said to have once done so. The story goes that an irate depositor, who had had a long argument with the local manager, arrived with a wheelbarrow and the demand that he be given his bank balance in dollars. After further negotiations, during which the doors were closed, a compromise was agreed to and the bank re-opened. Perhaps it was this drastic reminder of their slender resources that persuaded the directors to send Oakden off to found the Union Bank in London!

The Union Bank was merged with the Bank of Australasia in 1951 to become the Australia and New Zealand Bank.

Union Bank of Australia, Melbourne.

Sands, Kenny & C? Melbourne.   Sands & Kenny, Sydney.

82 This, the youngest of the Victorian Banks, was founded in 1858, with a local proprietary of 1250 shareholders. Its capital is £1,000,000, of which £212,407 is paid up, the amount of notes in circulation on 31st March, £191,114, its liabilities on 31st of March, 1861, were £665,310 14s. 6d., and its assets at same period £877,717 14s. 6d. At the last half-yearly meeting it declared a dividend at the rate of 6 per cent per annum.

An Australian writer looking for material on which to base a comedy-drama, might do worse than read the story surrounding the foundation of the now powerful and dignified National Bank of Australasia Ltd, which today has 706 branches in Australia, of which 240 are in Victoria.

Alexander Gibb, one of the principals in a move to create a new bank to be called the Colonial Bank of Australia, was bitterly disappointed when the bank was founded and he was not appointed its manager; with three other trustees he had ridden out to the gold centres to sell shares to subscribers who included Carboni Raffaelo, the Italian who later wrote about his part in the Eureka Stockade. In 1857, Gibb issued a prospectus for an entirely new bank—the National—and on 16 November, he accompanied 'Orator' McEachern on the coach to Ballarat, where they hoped to sell shares. McEachern was paid £2 2s. a day and all expenses.

The miners at that time were paying anything from 15 to 70 per cent interest on loans and they ignored appeals to buy shares; they wanted loans, not shares. Moreover other local banks promised to pay interest on current accounts. Then just as Gibb was about to admit defeat, he met Andrew Ross Cruickshank, wealthy pastoralist and merchant, who decided to back the new bank and take over the old Oriental Bank Corporation building in Queen Street.

Gibb presumed he would be general manager but on 31 August 1858 Daniel Hughes was appointed at £2,000 a year. Gibb refused to hand over the books and Hughes had to arrange to break open the safe. On Saturday 2 September Gibb applied for an injunction against the opening of the bank but he was too late; on Monday at 8 a.m. the National Bank opened to the buzz of excited comment from hundreds of sightseers. At 9 a.m., to the delight of many, the bank was closed on a Court order. Despite this reprieve for Gibb, the bank opened on the following Thursday (7 October). The Court decided that the board was properly constituted and that Hughes could not be removed.

Money was raised to provide a petition to Parliament to depose Hughes but Cruickshank felt so confident that he went to Adelaide to found a new branch. He overstayed his stipulated time and suddenly, on 2 December, a majority of directors voted against Hughes and Cruickshank. Hughes however locked up the books. Cruickshank on his return convened another meeting at which a fight began. Brown, one of the directors, ran to the window and shouted 'come and protect your property'. Previously-alerted shareholders did so and their bursting suddenly into the room made the usually cool Cruickshank lose his head; he shouted 'I do resign!' He added that he severed his connection with the bank there and then. The bank now had two boards, but a court action resulted in a verdict for the shareholders against Hughes on 29 January 1859. He claimed £10,000 damages but received only £500.

But although Hughes had been suspended, Gibb was never appointed but was granted rather mean compensation. Cruickshank died a few days later on 10 February, 1859. By that time the bank had moved its premises to 327 Collins Street where it leased premises later taken over by a hotel. However, this taking over of a bank site by a hotel in Collins Street did not establish a precedent. Today very few hotels remain in the street but there are more than thirty banks.

National Bank of Australasia, Melbourne.

Sands, Kenny & Co. Melbourne   Sands & Kenny, Sydney

THE BANK OF AUSTRALASIA, MELBOURNE

The Bank of Australasia was incorporated by Royal Charter in 1835, and the first Branch in Victoria was opened in Melbourne on the 28th August, 1838. It has a capital of £900,000, with a guarantee fund of £200,000 in addition to the reserved profits, amounting to £115,043. The note circulation in the Colony of Victoria, for the quarter ending 31st March, 1861, was £341,437. Total liabilities £1,732,837, and total assets £2,024,881. The Corporation has branches and agencies in every town of importance in this as well as in the neighbouring colonies of New South Wales, Queensland, Tasmania, and South Australia.

In June, 1838, two young men, David MacArthur and John Dunbar, officials of the newly-formed Bank of Australasia, were about to leave Sydney to open a branch at Bathurst when their directors learned from Governor George Gipps that they could anticipate getting government business if they opened a branch in Melbourne at the newly founded Port Phillip settlement. At the last moment then, changing their destination almost casually, MacArthur and Dunbar set off in the cutter 'Ranger', provided by Her Majesty's Government, with £3,000 in coin, two fierce bulldogs and an armed guard.

On their arrival in Melbourne the bankers rented a four-roomed cottage at the north-west corner of Queen Street and Flinders Lane. Two rooms 11 by 9 feet were used for their banking activities, while the other two were fitted up as living quarters. The grounds around the small cottage were cleared to allow the dogs to see and be seen and thus to protect the building more effectively. The valuable cash box, with its defective locks, was always placed between the beds of the two young bank officers. On the 28 August, 1838, the Bank of Australasia opened its doors for business and David MacArthur took the first step in a long and successful career which ultimately took him to the position of the bank's chief executive officer.

The building shown was erected in Collins Street, diagonally opposite the then Market Place, later the site of the Western Market and now the home of the huge National Mutual Building. The original block, 50 by 139 feet, had been bought for £1,000 to provide more permanent premises, which were taken over on 31 August, 1840. A new one-storey building on the west, that is the left-hand, side of the original two-storey building, was added as a new banking chamber in 1852. This building gave its name to Bank Place, a small lane leading through to the attractive Mitre Tavern. The Wesleyan Parsonage, a smaller two-storey building shown on the extreme right stood, with its chapel, on the north-west corner of Queen and Collins Streets.

An interesting reversal of policy was that the Union Bank, which had been founded in England in 1837 to combat the competition of the Bank of Australasia, merged with that bank in 1951 to become the Australia and New Zealand Bank with 561 branches, 121 of them in Victoria.

The Bank of Australasia, Melbourne.

Sands Kenny & Co. Melbourne.   Sands & Kenny. Sydney.

MELBOURNE SAVINGS BANK

To correct the erroneous impressions of the improvident habits of the people of Victoria, which obtained currency at a time when the discovery of gold in this colony unhinged men's minds and seemed to obviate the necessity for the exercise of prudence and frugality on the part of our population, it is only necessary to refer to the number of depositors in the various Savings Banks in Victoria, and the aggregate amount of the balances at their credit. At the Melbourne Savings' Bank, represented (together with the offices of the Board of Commissioners of Savings' Banks) on the opposite page, there were, on the 30th April, 1861, 6,647 depositors' accounts open, with an aggregate amount at their credit of £344,612 10s. 10d. Besides the Savings Banks in Melbourne, there are also Savings Banks at Geelong, Portland, Belfast, Castlemaine, Sandhurst, Ballarat, Maryborough, and Kyneton. The total number of depositors in all the Savings Banks in Victoria, on the 30th of April, 1861, was 11,564, and the aggregate amount at their credit £551,018 10s. 3d. A comparison of the most recent returns with those published in previous years, shows that that portion of the community for whose especial benefit these institutions have been established are availing themselves freely of their advantages, and that there is a steady increase in the number of depositors and in the amount of deposits. The rate of interest allowed on depositors' accounts open at the yearly balance on the 30th June, is 4 per cent, and the Commissioners of Savings Banks, who exercise a general control over the management of these institutions, and to whom is intrusted the investment of the entire Savings Banks funds, invest them, as far as practicable, in the Government securities of the colony.

The plan to set back this bank 16½ feet from the corner of Flinders Lane and Market Street, which accounts for the greater width of Flinders Lane at this point, was originally devised to give vehicles easier access to the Western Market on the block opposite. This explains why the engraving shows a barrow loaded with produce, probably oranges for one of the stalls.

The Bank Commissioners intended that no more than £4,000 should be spent on the building, but when tenders were called for the winning design by Sawyer and Purchas, none was received for less than £10,000, and ultimately Craven Brothers were awarded the contract for £10,800.

For years after its opening on 22 June 1858, the bank was regarded as one of the showplaces of Melbourne and, with additions made in 1884 and 1890, it remained the head office until 1912, when it was sold to the Melbourne Harbour Trust for £22,500— exclusive of the value of the site, which was Crown Land. The building remained until 1929 when it was demolished to make way for the present Harbour Trust building opened in 1931.

The parent of the Melbourne Savings' Bank was the Savings Bank of Port Phillip whose first branch was opened in Melbourne on 1 January 1842 with Charles Joseph La Trobe as one of its trustees. By 1850 another three branches had been added but in 1853, after Port Phillip District had become the colony of Victoria, the government transferred the administration of these branches to Commissioners, but insisted that each branch operate as a separate bank bearing the name of its locality—hence the Melbourne Savings' Bank. This arrangement was never satisfactory because no effective executive power was given to the local trustees who were gradually replaced by managers, thus establishing a pattern which suggested a single organisation with branches.

Finally in 1912, after an earlier battle for the control of Post Office Savings' Banks which threatened the existence of the original Savings banks, all branches of both banks were amalgamated as the State Savings Bank of Victoria. In effect, then, the Melbourne Savings' Bank was the link between our earliest Victorian savings bank open for a few hours each week, and the modern giant with about 500 branches and more than 700 agencies.

Melbourne Savings Bank

Sands Kenny & C.° Melbourne — Sands & Kenny Sydney

MELBOURNE EXCHANGE

88 This building, which owes its erection to private enterprise, in addition to its commercial uses, is occupied as the central station of the Electric Telegraph, by whose agency Melbourne is brought into communication with every town of importance in the colony and with the cities of Sydney and Adelaide, the capitals of the neighbouring colonies of New South Wales and South Australia. A submarine cable likewise connects Victoria with the island of Tasmania, but an accident has interrupted for a time the intercourse thus established. The magnitude of the commerce of this colony, the bulk of which is necessarily transacted by the merchants of Melbourne, may be inferred from the following figures, derived from the statistics annually published by the Government. The total value of the imports for the year ending the 31st of December, 1859, was £15,622,891; and of the exports during the same period £13,867,859. The number of vessels clearing from the port in that year was 1,716, with an aggregate tonnage of 603,111, and manned by 30,242 seamen. Gold and wool, of course, constitute the staple article of export, the quantity of the former shipped being 2,280,950 ounces, of the estimated value of £9,122,037, while coined gold was exported to the extent of £1,304,992, of which amount England received £543,052, Ceylon £138,158, and Mauritius £356,878. Of wool the exports were 21,660,295 lbs, of the estimated value of £1,656,950.

This building stood on the south side of Flinders Lane on the present site of the State Electricity Commission offices between Market and William Streets, but the first office of the Electric Telegraph Company was a tiny two-roomed shed on the north-east corner of William and Bourke Streets. From this office ran, in 1854, a single strand of wire strung along tall bare poles. The first message was sent on 3 March 1854 to where an operator sat in a cemetery—later the site of the Victoria Market—receiving the Morse signals being sent from the shed half a mile away. On 1 May 1854, the first official message was sent from Melbourne to Williamstown. The tariff was 2s. 6d. for ten words, with 3d. for every additional word. However, the name, address and signature were sent free. Before the Electric Telegraph was officially opened, a most important message was received from Williamstown where it had just arrived by sea mails: the news that Britain had declared war on Russia and was sending a force to the Crimea. 'Captain Wise was there', said the first telegraph manager, T. R. James, 'and when the message was read out he called for three cheers.' Captain Wise was later killed at Eureka.

Governor La Trobe was a frequent visitor to the first office and as there was only one stool, for the operator, the Governor had to stand as he watched operations. When the Electric Exchange was moved to the building depicted, the accommodation was shared with businessmen—such as William Hoseason, coal merchant; J. Sherry, a commission agent; and Alfred White, customs house agent.

That remarkable man Hugh Culling Childers (subsequently Britain's Chancellor of the Exchequer) claimed in 1866 in a letter to Prime Minister William Gladstone, that he was 'the originator of the system of government telegraph services in Australia'. Whether or not that is true, Childers as Victoria's Collector of Customs gave every encouragement to Samuel McGowan, a young Canadian who came to Melbourne in 1853, with three telegraph sets and ten miles of wire. McGowan had hoped to found a private telegraph company but Childers recommended to the colonial government that the telegraph should be part of the Post Office, and that even money orders should be paid by telegraph. He arranged for McGowan's appointment as the first superintendent. 'I remember the Governor of New South Wales, Sir William Denison', Childers said, 'laughing at my telegraph folly.'

Melbourne Exchange

Sands, Kenny & Co. Melbourne . Sands & Kenny, Sydney.

TEMPLE COURT, MELBOURNE

This extensive pile of buildings comprises a double range of offices communicating with Chancery Lane in the rear. The offices are chiefly occupied by members of the legal profession, and as there is some probability of the Law Courts being removed from the remote and inconvenient positions in which they now stand to a vacant site immediately opposite Temple Court, the latter edifice is likely to become as much frequented by visitors in Victoria as Westminster Hall in London, or the Four Courts in Dublin are by those who are prosecuting or defending actions at law.

When the Temple Court was thus pictured, Melbourne's Law Courts were near where the gaol once stood in Russell Street nearly opposite the present police headquarters. On the hill here public executions were once carried out. 'Look', said an early pioneer to his young son, 'it is hanging day on the hill, and the number of bright parasols slanting above the crowd is something astonishing.' Many years later, on 11 November 1880 5,000 people waited outside the Melbourne Gaol's twenty feet high wall running around the same hill, to hear that Australia's most famous bushranger, Ned Kelly, had been hanged despite many petitions for leniency.

But three years before that, in 1877, a fine building for the main law courts had been commenced on a two-acre site on another hill at the corner of William and Lonsdale Streets instead of on the 'vacant site immediately opposite Temple Court' which had once been the Western Market. In 1841, when the first gaol was removed from opposite where Temple Court later stood, La Trobe had suggested the erection of 'substantial and well-designed public edifices'. But controversy about plans for the new Law Courts lasted so long that thirty-six years had gone by before the contract for the building, on a different site, had been let for £250,000.

Built in the once fashionable western part of the city, the Law Courts are in Renaissance style. The maze of corridors, passages and vestibules include a number of little known stairways which lead directly from courts to judges' chambers. The three entrances to the Courts are flanked by fine ornamental lamps. The main door is surmounted by an escutcheon bearing the Royal Arms carved in stone and, high above, the traditional figure of Justice holds a sword but her eyes are unbandaged. Sir Redmond Barry persuaded the authorities that Justice should be wide-eyed, but not incredulously innocent.

The lawyers eventually moved to Selborne Chambers in Bourke Street, and then in 1964 to the new Owen Dixon Chambers in William Street opposite the more imposing of the Law Courts' two facades. Thus Temple Court never really achieved its object. Today it is the home of stockbrokers and a large group of insurance companies, sitting on the site of three blocks bought by C. H. Ebden for less than £150 in the first land sales in 1835 and sold, it is reported for £10,000 in 1840.

Happily the site's early association with the city has not been completely forgotten. A beautifully designed mosaic in the entrance hall of the present Temple Court shows eight of Victoria's outstanding personalities and eight unnamed Aborigines. The eight white men are John Batman, Edward Henty, William Lonsdale, William Russell, Robert Hoddle, Sir Richard Bourke, Charles La Trobe and, appropriately, John Pascoe Fawkner, who dearly loved a fight, who had been a 'bush lawyer' in Tasmania, and who once admitted that he wished he could have had the education to have 'taken up Law'.

Temple Court, Melbourne.

Sands, Kenny & Co. Melbourne — Sands & Kenny, Sydney.

MELBOURNE HOSPITAL

The Melbourne Hospital, like the city in which it has been instituted, arose from very small beginnings, the earliest Infirmary having consisted of a two-roomed log hut. In 1846 the foundation-stone of a portion of the present edifice was laid, and additions were made to the original structure from time to time until it assumed its present magnitude, and has become an institution of which the colony has justly reason to be proud. The revenues of the Hospital are derived from an annual grant by the Legislature of £13,000, which is made conditionally on a sum equal to the third of such grant being raised by voluntary contribution. In round numbers, about 3,000 in, and 8,000 out patients annually receive relief from this establishment, which is managed by a Committee, elected annually. The medical staff consists of eight Physicians and eight Surgeons, whose services are honorary, besides a Resident House-Surgeon, three Assistants and two Dispensers. The Hospital contains upwards of 300 beds, besides the necessary apartments for the resident officers. It is erected on a spacious and elevated plot of ground, granted for the purpose by the Government of the day, in the immediate vicinity of other reserves set apart for public purposes. Apart from the benevolent uses it fulfils, the institution is of great value in the absence of any school in Melbourne, as an auxiliary to surgical science. The Hospital will bear comparison, indeed, in nearly every respect, with the best appointed and most liberally endowed institutions of a similar character in the Old World.

In the first year of the Melbourne Hospital one of its most hated regulations was that no person could be automatically treated as an in-patient but had to be recommended by a contributor of £2 2s. per year who, in his turn had to guarantee that he would remove a patient who died or pay forty shillings towards the expenses of burial. The contributor also had to certify that his friend had three shirts and three pairs of stockings. The guarantee was no idle formality. In that year (1848) of the 75 patients treated, 22 died, 2 died before they were admitted, 3 were made out-patients, 12 were relieved, 32 were cured and 4 left of their own accord.

Those were primitive days in any hospital. In 1847, James Egan of Campaspe shattered his right wrist and hand when his gun burst. His agonising journey to the city took four days. On arrival, he was made comfortable with brandy and opium. Next day, after more brandy and opium, his arm was amputated below the elbow—the first man in Victoria to be operated on under anaesthetic. Three days later the stitches were removed, the patient was given two bottles of stout a day and, after caustic and lime treatment, the tough bushman was on his way home within the month.

This operation took place in the second of the two hospitals which preceded the building at Swanston Street. The first, established in 1840, was a small brick cottage in Little Collins Street and the second a more commodious two-storey building in Bourke Street. The foundation stone of the Swanston Street hospital was laid on 20 March 1846, for the good and sensible reason that the second Princes Bridge was also being founded that day and that therefore the same procession could be used for both occasions. And what a procession it was! It spilled from 'end to end of Collins Street' and was led by the Chief Constable on horseback, Mounted and Border Police, followed by schoolchildren and Temperance Bands with Superintendent Charles La Trobe sandwiched in the centre 'on horseback, in vice-regal costume with a splendid flowing White Plume with Sword'.

When the new building was opened two years later, a contemporary wrote that 'it looked like a red rookery perched in the centre of a waste of bush with large half-charred tree trunks here and there'. However, by the time this drawing was made the area had been improved, and the hospital underlined its efficiency by announcing in 1855 that of 1,605 in-patients, only 276 had died. Unimpressive as these statistics may seem today, the 'Melbourne', as it had come to be called, could be proud of its services as the only public hospital working during the crowded years of the gold rush.

The Melbourne Hospital buildings that began at Swanston Street and expanded along the Lonsdale Street frontage as far as Russell Street have become the Queen Victoria Memorial Hospital. The 'Melbourne'—now the Royal Melbourne Hospital—is situated in Parkville; this massive complex of buildings is a far cry from the cottage of 1840.

Melbourne Hospital.

Sands, Kenny & Co Melbourne — Sands & Kenny Sydney.

COLLEGIATE GRAMMAR SCHOOL, ST. KILDA

94 The site upon which this collegiate-looking edifice stands, was granted by the Government under Sir Charles Hotham, and includes fifteen acres within its limits. The school itself which was designed by Messrs Webb and Taylor, was erected at a cost of £20,000, about two-thirds of which amount were voted by the Legislature, while the residue was made up by private subscriptions. It was opened in April, 1858, and is capable of receiving 300 pupils. The general control of the establishment is vested in a council; but its more immediate superintendence is confided to Dr Bromby, the Head Master, whose scholastic attainments and high personal character admirably qualify him for the responsible task. Although professedly a Church of England School, it is not exclusively so, and scholars of any denomination are admitted without being required to attend the theological lectures. The education and discipline resemble those of the public schools in the mother country, and several of the students have gone up with credit to the University, to which it will prove a valuable adjunct. In the immediate vicinity of three public parks, and the Botanical Gardens, at an inconsiderable distance from the sea, the situation of the Grammar School is a very favourable one, and, when completed by the erection of a tower, the structure will be an ornament to the site, and will vie in point of architectural beauty with some of the collegiate establishments of Great Britain.

This school, generally known as Melbourne Grammar School, was opened on 7 April 1858 but it really began ten years earlier as the dream of the first Anglican Bishop of Melbourne, Charles Perry, who was an old Harrovian. As soon as Bishop Perry arrived in Melbourne in 1848, he began planning to build a school which he believed would one day rival the great public schools of Britain. The first step was taken when the diocesan school of St Peter's, Eastern Hill, was established by Richard Hale Budd—educated at Rugby— who also had a great admiration for the English public school tradition. When Budd resigned in 1854, Perry saw the small establishment developing into a great Church of England Grammar School.

His hopes were heightened in the same year when Parliament voted £20,000 for the establishment of denominational grammar schools. More than half of this amount was allocated to the Church of England which, with its further share of another £15,000 government grant two years later, had by 1856 £21,000 to its credit. Of this amount £14,000 was set aside for Melbourne Grammar and £7,000 for Geelong Grammar, forty miles from Melbourne. The foundation stone of the Melbourne school was laid that year and the fine bluestone buildings were occupied on 7 April 1858.

Dr Bromby the first headmaster began a tradition by his personal example, as a man who loved games and relied more on moral strength than strict discipline. Moreover he was a gifted preacher, of great courage and scholarship. When he resigned in 1874, he handed over to another outstanding man, Edward Ellis Morris, who introduced the prefect system, a fine school library and the first school magazine in Melbourne. He was only 32 when he was appointed.

Today, the original bluestone buildings blend with the many new additions, and the two old headmasters would find much to delight them, not the least of which is the school's reputation for turning out fine scholars and good sportsmen. The sports tradition was already alive in 1858 when Bromby was headmaster and the first game of Australian Rules football was played between Melbourne Grammar and Scotch College.

Collegiate Grammar School, St Kilda.

Sands Kenny & Cº Melbourne   Sands & Kenny, Sydney

ST. PATRICK'S COLLEGE, MELBOURNE

The Roman Catholics constitute a numerically large and socially influential portion of the population of Victoria, and the educational and benevolent institutions belonging to this body are liberally supported. The Diocesan College, which occupies the south-eastern angle of the reserve upon which the new Cathedral is in course of erection upon the Eastern Hill, is conducted by the Rev. Dr Barry and a staff of able Professors. The education imparted is such as to qualify students for the priesthood, the learned professions, or the pursuits of commerce, and the public examinations prove both the efficiency of the system employed and the high attainments of many of those who are receiving instruction in this establishment.

In the year this drawing was published, 1862, the history of St Patrick's College was interrupted by bankruptcy. It was revived in 1865 but just over a century later, in 1968, it ceased to be a school and became the Catholic Services Centre for the archdiocese of Melbourne. Before the foundation stone of St Patrick's College was laid in December 1854, there had been a high school for boys in a hall attached to St Francis' Church; it had been established by Bishop Goold in May, 1849. Soon afterwards, the bishop set up a seminary for training priests in a part of the same building; until 1853, it was under the charge of Father Gerald Ward who later founded the St Vincent de Paul Orphanage in South Melbourne. When St Patrick's College opened in East Melbourne in 1855, the high school and seminary were transferred there. The first president of the college was a Franciscan priest, Dr L. B. Shiel, who had succeeded Father Ward as head of the school and seminary at St Francis'. When Dr Shiel retired in 1858, an Englishman, Mr Patrick Whyte, became headmaster. He was succeeded by the Rev. Dr John Barry D.D., under whose regime the school temporarily closed down.

Dr Barry was a distinguished classics and Hebrew scholar and a fine teacher but a poor businessman. On 9 August 1862 distress warrants had been issued on the college furniture and effects for debts and loans amounting to hundreds of pounds. Soon the college had to shut down, bankrupt. It came to life again on Monday 9 October when the school reopened in charge of two Jesuit priests invited by Bishop Goold to come to Melbourne from the Irish province of the Society of Jesus. They were Father Joseph Lentaigne (Rector of the college), and Father William Kelly. Father Lentaigne once said that 'the little colonials preferred play to study, but later showed that they could study as well'. In 1867, Father Lentaigne composed and a pupil, young Claude Keogh, recited a Latin Sapphic ode as part of the school's contribution to the combined Speech Night of the Victorian public schools—their gesture of welcome to the Duke of Edinburgh. 'It was probably the only classical ode His Excellency received', reported the Melbourne Argus *'As the ode was in Latin, we do not think many understood it . . . it was certainly a great day.' The school's early speech nights showed the versatility of the St Patrick's boys—as, for example, on 19 December 1870. In addition to speeches, music recitals, callisthenics, exhibitions of fencing and demonstrations in chemistry, the boys took part in a number of exercises in arithmetic and languages in which they proposed and answered questions.*

The school remained solvent, but it must have been a hard struggle at times; although the fees were small enough at a nominal £3 a quarter, they were further reduced by allowances for more than one in the family, needy parents and bad debts. Probably the average income was only £7 a year from each pupil. Nevertheless the college grew so fast that accommodation for boarders became inadequate and the grounds too small for sports and games. By the 1880s therefore, the boarders were transferred to the Jesuits' new school, Xavier College, Kew. St Patrick's waived its right to membership of the Public Schools Association in favour of Xavier.

St Patrick's College, Melbourne.

Sands, Kenny & Co. Melbourne   Sands & Kenny, Sydney

SUBURBAN RAILWAY BRIDGE, HAWTHORN

The Suburban Railway connects, in an easternly direction, Melbourne with Hawthorne, distance three and a half miles, passing through the thickly populated Municipality of Richmond. Branching southerly from Richmond at nearly right angles to the Hawthorn line, it crosses the river at South Yarra, and passing through Prahran terminates at Windsor. The original scheme was to extend it to Brighton, but that is for the present in abeyance. There are six miles of line completed, constructed at a cost, including rolling stock and buildings, of £400,000.

The engraving here shown represents the bridge over the Yarra on the Hawthorne line, and also furnishes a glimpse of a public reserve known by the most unhappy title of the 'Survey Paddock'—with nearly equal appropriateness it might be called a brickfield. The reserve is delightfully sequestered and the scenery exceedingly beautiful, the ground forming a succession of agreeable undulations profusely embellished with trees, and though in all but one hundred and ninety acres, from the unsuspected windings of the Yarra Yarra, and there being a river frontage of two miles and a half, an illusion is produced that the extent embraced is far greater than exists in reality. Recently twenty-five acres within the reserve have been granted by the Government to the Horticultural Society of Victoria, for the purpose of acclimatising and cultivating fruits, flowers, and vegetables, on a plan conformable with similar institutes in Great Britain, Ireland, and America.

The Hawthorn Railway Bridge would probably have been the oldest surviving bridge over the Yarra if the Schomberg under the command of the famous skipper 'Bully Forbes' had not been wrecked on Boxing Day 1855 at Curdie's River on the south-west coast of Victoria, near Warrnambool. Unfortunately the iron bridge intended for the Hawthorn line went down in the wreck, and the bridge shown here was not opened until April 1861 when an hourly train service, between 8.10 a.m. and 6.10 p.m., was introduced between Melbourne and Hawthorn.

This was virtually only an extension of the line, because eight months earlier, in September 1860, the Melbourne line ran as far as the Picnic Station on the Richmond side of the river. Seven trains were available daily, between 8.20 a.m. and 5.20 p.m., and the fares ranged from 9d. single and 1s. 3d. return, first class, to 6d. and 9d. second class.

Hawthorn was one of the earliest Melbourne suburbs and was settled by people who either could not afford home sites in Melbourne or Richmond or wished 'to get out of the bustling city to the peaceful quiet of the country'. Its original name is a matter of argument. Some claim that it was named after Lieutenant Hawthorne (spelt with an 'e' as in two places in the original legend to this engraving), a naval officer and friend of Robert Hoddle, the Surveyor-General who laid out the broad streets of Melbourne. Others say that it was named after the lovely hawthorn blossom for which the district was famous.

The twenty-five acres reserved for the Royal Horticultural Society of Victoria is still set aside, although it now belongs to the Burnley College of Horticulture which carries on the traditions of the first society with valuable research work.

Suburban Railway Bridge, Hawthorn.

Sands, Kenny & Co. Melbourne   Sands & Kenny, Sydney.

REVD. IRVING HETHERINGTON'S SCOTCH CHURCH AND MANSE, MELBOURNE

This Church and Manse occupies one of the finest sites in the city of Melbourne, at the intersection of Collins and Russell Streets. The Church was erected in 1841, and has been lately extensively remodelled and finished with a tower and spire; the Manse was erected in 1852. The Rev. Irving Hetherington is the Minister. This is the first Presbyterian Church erected in the colony, and is distinguished as the scene of the Union of the Presbyterian Churches in April, 1859, and as the Place of meeting of the General Assembly of the Presbyterian Church of Victoria.

Scots Church will always be associated with its first minister, James Forbes, who arrived in Melbourne in January 1838 as a young man of 25, to become the city's first permanent minister. His first church was a tiny place that cost £109 to build opposite St James' Church in Collins Street beyond William Street. When the church received a grant of a block of two acres at the corner of Russell and Collins Streets there were grumbles that this site was 'too far out of town'.

The first building on the new site was weatherboard but in May 1839 a move was made to add a brick building which was to serve as a school house and church and also be available for 'all useful purposes' including the first town lectures. It cost £524 and stood on the site of Georges. Meantime efforts went on to raise funds for the handsome church which was planned for the site on which Scots Church now stands. On 22 January 1841 the foundation stone was laid for a church to cost £4,000 and accommodate 600 people. Among the contributions to the funds was £6 by the popular Catholic priest, Father Geoghegan, who had handed a £5 and a £1 note to a trustee. When his generosity was publicised, Father Geoghegan protested that he had given two £1 notes. It was proved that he had made a mistake and he was offered £4, but he refused to accept it.

The day of the foundation ceremony was very wet, but hundreds of Presbyterians assembled at 11 o'clock in the morning to listen to their Minister and Elders, and to join in singing the 122nd Psalm. A large parchment scroll, the three newspapers of the day, the Gazette, Patriot and Herald, as well as Kerr's Port Phillip Directory 1841 were deposited with the foundation stone. The building was opened for service on 3 October, 1841.

Five years later, the effects of the internal dissension which rocked the church in Scotland, were reflected in the resignation of the Rev. James Forbes. After carrying on services in the Mechanics' Institution (today the Atheneum building), he was offered a block of land at the corner of Swanston and Little Lonsdale Streets, where he built his John Knox Church as the headquarters of this new congregation, the Free Presbyterian Church of Victoria. A school was added which became so popular that a larger one had to be built at the back of the church.

James Forbes died on 4 August 1851 after thirteen years of service to the religious and educational life of the community. By 1863 a new church had replaced the John Knox building, by 1879 the congregation had been dissolved and in 1873 his Scots Church had been demolished and the present handsome building erected by David Mitchell, father of Dame Nellie Melba who often sang in the choir. Chalmers' Free Church School, then known as the Melbourne Academy, which had been inspired by Forbes, became Scotch College in its East Melbourne period. The Presbyterian Church in Melbourne had been re-united.

Revd Irving Hetherington's Scotch Church and Manse, Melbourne.

Sands, Kenny & C.º Melbourne ., Sands & Kenny, Sydney.

WESLEYAN CHURCH, MELBOURNE

One of the handsomest ecclesiastical structures, externally, and the most capacious internally, of which Melbourne can boast, is the edifice erected, in Lonsdale Street, East, by the members of the Wesleyan Denomination. The designs were prepared by Mr Reid, who is also the architect of the Melbourne Public Library; and although the situation is not sufficiently elevated to give full effect to the general appearance of the building, it constitutes one of the most picturesque features of our civic architecture; and the mediaeval aspect of the structure offers a startling contrast to the mean and modern character of most of the tenements in its immediate neighbourhood. The funds necessary for the erection of Wesley Church were obtained by the sale of a small allotment of land, formerly occupied by a Wesleyan Chapel, in one of the leading thoroughfares in Melbourne. Brought to the hammer, the land realized £40,000; although its original value, when the city was first laid out in 1837, would have fallen short of £50. According to the Census of 1854, the number of Wesleyan Methodists in Victoria was 15,284, having 26 places of worship, with 25 ministers, and 169 lay readers, lay preachers and mission agents; and at the end of 1859, the number of churches and chapels belonging to this persuasion had increased to 213, capable of seating 34,000 persons, and 6,000 children of Wesleyan Methodists were in attendance at the 74 denominational schools occupied by this body. It is worthy of remark that divine service was celebrated, for the first time in Victoria, by the Rev. Mr Orton, a Wesleyan Minister, who read the Church of England Liturgy and preached a sermon under some trees upon the summit of Batman's Hill, when as yet the site of the future city of Melbourne had not been defined.

Wesley Church was built on the third site occupied by the Methodist denomination in Melbourne. The first, donated by John Joseph Peers, was bought for £129 from John Batman, who paid £59 for it at land sales in November 1837. A small brick chapel, 30 by 16 feet, costing £100, was also donated by Peers. The church was opened in 1839 by the Rev. Joseph Orton. Mr Orton had been brought to Melbourne in 1836, and on 24 April had preached to a congregation which included in the front row 'a tall well-built Aboriginal wearing a cockaded hat with feathers, and pieces of cast-off military uniform. Next to him were Batman's Sydney Aborigines dressed in white trousers, shirts and black neckerchiefs. Standing beside the sophisticated Sydneyites were a handful of primitive Port Phillip Aborigines clad in possum skins.'

Soon the chapel became too small for the growing congregation. Once again Peers helped by persuading the government to grant the Methodists a half-acre site at the north-west corner of Queen and Collins Streets.

The small chapel on the first site at the north-western corner of Swanston Street and Flinders Lane later served as the kitchen of the Queen's Arms Hotel. The second site had been bought by Mr H. B. Bowman for £40 at the first Melbourne land sales in June 1837. However, Bowman had second thoughts about the value of the land—it is said that he dreamt he had paid too much for it—and he decided to forfeit the land and his £4 deposit. Twenty years later, the second church built on this site had become too small for the congregation and it decided to sell the land and use the money to build a handsome church in Lonsdale Street. The £40 block brought £40,000!

Wesleyan Church, Melbourne

Sands Kenny & Co. Melbourne   Sands & Kenny, Sydney

CHALMER'S CHURCH, MELBOURNE

The name and memory of the great Scottish divine are perpetuated by this church, with its adjacent manse and Scotch College contiguous, are finely placed upon the Eastern Hill, in the immediate vicinity of one of the public parks, the houses of Parliament, St Patrick's Cathedral and College, and the Treasury; while upon the same spacious reserve have been erected St Peter's Church (Episcopalian), an Unitarian Church, and the Chapel in which the German Lutherans celebrate divine worship. The Rev. Dr Cairns occupies the pulpit of Chalmers' Church; and the Presbyterian denomination, in point of numbers, rank third upon the list of the various religious bodies enumerated in the Census of the colony.

The great Scottish preacher and writer, Thomas Chalmers was warmly welcomed when he visited London in 1817. 'All the world is wild about Dr Chalmers', wrote an enthusiastic reporter. Seventeen years later arguments were raging about Chalmers. He had become the leader of the evangelical section of the Church of Scotland, determined that 'no minister shall be intruded into any parish contrary to the will of the congregation'. The arguments concerned the spiritual rights of the church and the dangers and abuses of Royal patronage.

On 18 May 1843 these differences split the church and 474 ministers under the leadership of Chalmers left the establishment to form the Free Church of Scotland. The breakaway movement spread far beyond the boundaries of Scotland. More than £3,000,000 was contributed by supporters in many parts of the world. But four years later, in 1847, Chalmers died. He had been working out a sustenance scheme for seceding ministers; after giving evidence in the House of Commons, he walked home and later was found dead in bed.

By that time many new churches had been founded. One was the Free Presbyterian Church of Australia Felix in Victoria, with the brilliant James Forbes at its head. Forbes founded the John Knox church and was instrumental in founding Chalmers' Free Church with its Chalmers' Free Church School which became the Melbourne Academy and later Victoria's first public school, Scotch College. Forbes died in 1851 but the new denomination prospered. In 1852, the Free Church of Scotland sent out two clergymen and ten younger men to Australia to strengthen the movement. One of the preachers, Rev. Dr Adam Cairns was to be a force in the religious life of Melbourne for many years. He became the minister of Chalmers' Free Church, bringing with him his own prefabricated iron church which had cost £1,300. This was erected on the first site occupied by the church at 237 Spring Street, between Lonsdale and Little Lonsdale Streets. In September 1854, the church and its school were granted a two-acre site in Gipps Street between Parliament Place and Lansdowne Street. Here the congregation erected a handsome wooden structure which held 1,000 worshippers, but later the church shown here, a 'worthy stone edifice costing £8,000', replaced this building.

In 1859, after all the bitterness and dissention of the previous half century, several branches of the Presbyterian Church amalgamated and the Chalmers' Free Church became Chalmers' Church, the property of the united denomination. James Forbes' other church struggled on outside the United Presbyterian Movement. A new church was built on the same site in 1863, but funds were so short that many of the bricks in the old church were used in the new building. It was ultimately sold to the Church of Christ. Today, the name of that famous Melbourne preacher of Chalmers' Free Church, Dr Adam Cairns is commemorated by Cairns Memorial Presbyterian Church, in East Melbourne.

Chalmers' Church, Melbourne.

Young Kenny & Co. Melbourne. Sands & Kenny, Sydney.

MELBOURNE AND HOBSON'S BAY RAILWAY STATION, ST. KILDA

The construction of a branch of the Melbourne and Hobson's Bay Railway to St Kilda has virtually converted that watering-place into a suburb of Melbourne. Ten years ago St Kilda was a diminutive village, scarcely reclaimed from the bush, and accessible only by a devious and dangerous road. At the present time it includes a population equal to that of Gravesend. The Esplanade is fringed with elegant villas, and during the summer months the beach is enlivened on Sundays and holydays by shoals of visitors from Melbourne. Erected into a municipality, a short time back, the work of local improvement has been vigorously prosecuted in St Kilda, and as a large proportion of its population is composed of persons in affluent circumstances, the funds available for effecting these improvements have been easily raised, while they have been supplemented by grants-in-aid from the Legislature, in accordance with a practice which has prevailed ever since the introduction of the municipal system into Victoria. The railway, of which a view of the St Kilda Terminus is given on the opposite page, runs for some distance along the edge of a public park, which stretches halfway between Melbourne and the former place, and an extension of the line in an easterly direction connects St Kilda with Brighton, another watering-place a few miles further down the Bay. With whomsoever the name of this place originated, it is singularly inappropriate, for nothing can be more unlike the bleak and storm-beaten St Kilda of the Hebrides than its southern namesake, lying on the edge of a calm expanse of deep blue water and enveloped in a bland transparent atmosphere, which bears a much greater resemblance to that of Naples than to anything to be met with in the North of Europe.

The railway line between Melbourne and St Kilda was very popular at first. In the first six months to the end of October 1857, it carried more than 382,000 people; in the next six months the total was 512,933. The local people wanted the train; as one potential subscriber put it: '. . . we are tired of getting wet through or scorched in the broiling sun while we wait for unreliable omnibuses.' Moreover St Kilda Road was rough and at times dangerous. Not long before, five bushrangers had held up traffic on the road and bound their captives to trees.

But the councillors of the Albert Park and South Melbourne areas were anything but helpful towards the new railway. They grumbled about the costs and inconvenience of level crossings and about the effect of the railway embankment on the local drainage. But for the vigilance of the police, railway navvies and council employees would have attacked each other. There were legal arguments from which only lawyers profited; when this was realised the quarrels ceased and the laying down of the track was allowed to continue.

Shortly after the opening on 14 May 1857, the Argus reported: 'The St Kilda Railway is one of our greatest luxuries. All the world—that is Melbourne—lives out of town and St Kilda is on the bay . . . some passengers growl about the 9d. a day fare . . . nonetheless the trains are always crowded and, at holiday times, the passengers are numbered by the thousands and ten thousands.'

In the building shown, the platform is shorter than in the present station, but the main lines of the building remain unchanged. One feature has gone. When the line was opened, the Herald report mentioned 'a neat brick edifice, containing refreshment and waiting rooms for ladies and the indispensable accompaniment of a large bar and a pretty barmaid'. Alas, the bar and barmaid have long since disappeared.

Melbourne and Hobson's Bay Railway Station, S. Kilda

Sands, Kenny & Co. Melbourne. Sands & Kenny, Sydney.

MECHANICS' INSTITUTION, MELBOURNE

The Mechanics Institution and School of Arts, Collins Street, is one of the oldest Public Buildings in Melbourne, having been erected more than twenty years ago. It is supported by public subscription, aided by grants from the Public Treasury; the management is vested in a President, a Vice-President, and Committee of Management, who are all elected by the subscribers. The subscription is £1 a year, with a small entrance fee. A Reading Room, Lecture Hall, and Circulating Library are at the service of the subscribers. A payment of £10 entitles a person to become a Life Member. This building, for many years, contained the Temporary Offices of the Town Council; and many of the most important public meetings were, moreover, held in its public room. A number of clergymen, well known in the early days of Victoria, used it as a place of Public Worship. There have recently been conversaziones established in connexion with the Institution.

On 4 October 1839, a few members of the newly formed Union Benefit Society carried the following resolution: 'That a Mechanics' Institution be formed in Melbourne for the promotion of Science in this rising colony, particularly among the young . . . that and a public meeting for the formation of such an institution be held on the first Tuesday in November.'

The inaugural lecture was given by J. H. Osborne, a retired but active Presbyterian minister, who spoke about 'The Advantages of such an Institution'. The second lecture, on 'Agriculture', was the work of the versatile Judge Redmond Barry. The Rev. James Forbes spoke on 'Colonization', and George Arden, editor of the Gazette, chose a title which would have seemed far too wordy for today's newspapers: 'The Mechanical Agency of the Press in the Dissemination of General Knowledge'. After this auspicious beginning— and the enrolling of two hundred members—it came as a surprise that the government gave only qualified approval for a grant of land. The members decided that they would buy at the next land sales, and J. H. Osborne, the secretary, managed to get two blocks between Swanston and Russell Streets for £142 10s. each. One was retained for the Mechanics' Institution building which was erected in 1843; the other was later sold at a very good profit.

The new building was a 'substantial, two-storey red brick edifice' some feet above and away from the level of the steeply sloping Collins Street. In the winter all the approaches were muddy and dangerous; nevertheless many large crowds assembled in the building to attend gatherings which included some of the most important social, charitable and political events of the day. The second building, shown here, was built in 1857 and a third, built in 1872 with a facade added in 1885, was given its present name, the Athenaeum.

The Mechanics' Institution saw some exciting events; one of the most memorable was the election, on 17 June 1843, (in the days before separation) of the city's first parliamentary representative to the Legislative Council of New South Wales. The two contenders were the Mayor, Henry Condell, and Edward Curr, a great protagonist for the separation of Port Phillip District from New South Wales. The main polling booth was at the Mechanics' Institution and here drunks and partisans jostled each other as bulletins were posted each hour. The excitement became hotter and Captain Dana rode in with his native police; then the police magistrate, Major St John, never noted for his tact, pulled a copy of the Riot Act from his pocket and read it to the milling crowd, who replied with jeers.

It was felt to be a dangerous moment, but the troopers maintained a sense of the occasion and remained impassive, apart from a little 'flashy pantomine' when some hooligans tried to unhorse them. Then a rumour spread that some Condellites were being attacked; the crowd split up into rival groups, racing through the town, breaking windows and insulting anyone who disagreed with them. But no one was seriously hurt and at the Mechanics' Institution the election result was announced: Henry Condell, with 295 votes to Curr's 261, had become Melbourne's first parliamentarian.

OFFICE
DOMESTICS.

MECHANICS INSTITUTION

SCHOOL OF ARTS

Mechanics' Institution, Melbourne

Sands, Kenny & Co Melbourne   Sands & Kenny, Sydney

BANK OF VICTORIA, GEELONG

110 A Branch of the Metropolitan Establishment; each of the Melbourne Banks having a similar offshoot in this town, a circumstance which is to some extent an indication of the magnitude of its mercantile transactions.

The Bank of Victoria was probably one of the most successful of Victorian gold rush banks and, in a sense, the only truly Victorian bank. But its name has not only disappeared, but disappeared because it was taken over by a New South Wales bank, the Commercial Banking Company of Sydney.

When the Bank of Victoria was founded in 1853, there was only limited outlet for investment by successful miners. A few small businesses offered opportunities but land in the city, which should have been available for investment, was so scarce and the demand so great that government auctions saw prices rice to £200 a foot—more than in London or New York. Speculators made immense profits; land and building companies mushroomed overnight.

Many banks were doing well at this time, especially the Bank of Victoria whose leaders, wealthy investor Henry Miller and parliamentarian William Westgarth, had aroused local feeling by accusing banks whose headquarters were outside Australia of grabbing large profits to which they were not entitled. 'We object', they shouted, 'to watching foreign banks which feed off the prosperity of this thriving colony.' When a rumour had gone around that English banks were about to begin buying gold, a meeting of Melbourne merchants not only decided to form their own bank but took up all the 20,000 shares offered at £50 each. 'Money' Miller, who had earlier refused to join the project, was at the meeting and took up the last 500 shares offered. He became the bank's first chairman and it justified the nickname Melbourne had given the able Henry Miller; branch after branch was opened in Victoria as the bank moved into the gold centres, buying gold at fair prices which still represented fine investments. Although the official price of gold was £3 17s. 10½d. the price paid by private buyers had averaged £3 and on the diggings as little as £2 5s. was accepted. One of the reasons for this was that, until late 1852, no one knew whether Victorian gold was of the best quality. When it was confirmed that it was, the private buyers, who had made huge profits, were quickly driven out of the market by banks like the Victoria.

For a while, no one dared to found another local bank. 'Mr Henry Miller is King of Victoria', wrote the Age, 'and not a merchant . . . dares squeak without his permission.' Later in that decade, however, two new local banks, the National and the Colonial, were founded and, after expanding into other Australian States, merged sixty years later. By 1878, there were suggestions that the Bank of Victoria, which had never opened branches outside Victoria, should amalgamate with the National, but Henry Miller refused to make the first move. It was not until 1927 that the 120 Victorian branches of the Victoria were taken over by the Commercial Banking Company of Sydney.

Miller and the Bank of Victoria had only one real defeat in their earliest days. Miller became chairman of a select committee which recommended that the Bank of Victoria become the official bank of the Government—but the Government would not agree.

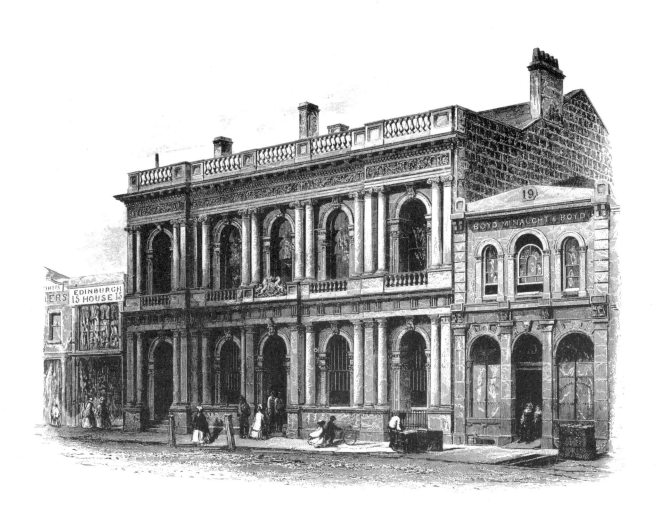

GEELONG GRAMMAR SCHOOL

112   This commodious structure, erected at a cost of £12,500, was opened in June, 1858.

The first constitution of Geelong Grammar School insisted that the headmaster 'shall be a clergyman of the Church of England and a graduate of Oxford, Cambridge, Dublin or Melbourne. He shall be appointed by the trustees and shall hold the office quam diu se bene gesserit. *He shall conduct the school at his own expense, and shall have the use of the school buildings, and receive the school fees, subject to deductions for repairs etc.' This was fixed by the trustees and shall be provided with house accommodation'.*

By 1860 the school was in such financial difficulties that it closed down and its first headmaster, the Rev. George Oakley Vance, resigned. It remained closed until 1863 when it was reconstituted by an act of the church assembly and reopened with John Bracebridge Wilson as its new headmaster. Wilson, who remained for thirty-three years, had taken his M.A. at St John's College, Cambridge. He was a great headmaster and some called him 'the Doctor Arnold of the Colonies', implying some comparison between the Rugby School of Arnold's day and Geelong Grammar under Wilson. Perhaps there was a similarity. When the Right Reverend J. F. Stretch, Bishop of Newcastle, recalled his first days at Geelong Grammar School, he said that in accordance with a school rule 'a big boy was told off to fight me and I was licked; but I fancy that I must have fought as well as I could, because I was not bothered much afterward'.

Bishop Stretch also recalled that he was one of the first six boys in the school to sit for the matriculation examination in 1869. He wrote: 'We were taken with all solemnity by the headmaster himself to Melbourne where we stayed at a quiet hotel. It was a most stupid, variegated and wearisome performance. Nine subjects—three a day. We went solemnly up to the University each day. By the last day, I was so tired, I went next to doing my worst with my best subject.'

Bishop Stretch belonged to a family which had many associations with Geelong Grammar. The original diocesan school was established by Archdeacon Stretch of St Paul's, Geelong, on 1 October 1855 at a house in Villamanta Street; the Rev. George Vance who was appointed to the school and who later became Geelong's first headmaster was the archdeacon's curate. The school remained at Villamanta Street for only a few months, then moved to larger premises in Skene Street, Geelong. The foundation stone was laid on 24 June 1857 by the Governor, Sir Henry Barkly, and the boys—100 pupils, of whom 41 were boarders—moved in on 15 April. Among the first pupils were two sons of the Archdeacon and among the staff three Vances—the headmaster, and two teachers, Rev. James Vance, a cousin, and W. F. Vance.

The school was officially opened on 24 June 1858. Sir Henry was expected to be present again but pleaded illness and the Geelong Advertiser *showed resentment: 'It had been confidently expected that Sir Henry Barkly, the Governor, would take part in the ceremony. Indeed he had accepted an invitation to do so but unfortunately His Excellency was prevented from carrying out his intention by a somewhat sudden indisposition, so it was said.'*

On the day, Bishop Perry conducted a special service which was followed by 'an elegant repast . . . . provided in the dining room' and a ball described as a 'very brilliant affair'. By the time Archdeacon Stretch proposed the toast to the absent governor, feelings had mellowed and his speech, 'punctuated by frequent laughter', was followed by enthusiastic drinking of the Governor's health with 'three times three'.

In 1914, the school moved to its present 380-acre site on the shores of Limeburners Lagoon, Corio Bay—eight miles from the centre of Geelong.

Geelong Grammar School.

Sands Kenny C° Melbourne . Sands & Kenny Sydney

114 Several of the handsomest commercial buildings in Geelong are erected in this street, which from its contiguity to the railway constitutes one of the principal thoroughfares of the place. The foundation of Geelong dates as far back as 1837, and the town was incorporated in 1849. An immense impulse was given to its growth and prosperity by the discovery of the gold-fields at Ballaarat, its imports, which had only been of the value of £60,423 in 1850, having risen to £1,705,522 in 1853, while its population, which was 8,291 only in 1851, has augmented to 20,115 in 1854.

In September 1851 the Cavanagh brothers arrived in Geelong from Ballarat with sixty pounds of gold. Geelong saw this as a promise of their future pre-eminence over Melbourne; the Ballarat goldfield was their goldfield and would enormously increase Geelong's trade and exports. In 1852, the Geelong and Melbourne Railway company was formed with a capital of £350,000 in the hope that this would attract additional shipping to Geelong, whence goods would be transported to Melbourne. But by the time this drawing was made, Geelong had lost all hope of overtaking Melbourne, despite the local increase in industry and agriculture, the beginning of Geelong wool sales, and the completion of a second channel through the harbour bar. This second channel began almost immediately to silt again so that Geelong's deep-water harbour was not as unrestricted as had been hoped. Moreover, a new railway line between Ballarat and Melbourne had been opened in the same year, 1862, thus enabling traffic to bypass Geelong, whose railway was used to bring goods from Melbourne. At the back of all this was political manoeuvring to ensure that Melbourne remained capital. A commercial map was even issued showing, quite falsely, that Ballarat was closer to Melbourne than Geelong.

Geelong was first spelled 'Jillong', a native word the translation of which offers the historical researcher a choice of 'peace of the native companion', 'white sea bird' and 'place of a cliff'. Although the first settlers made their homes on the Barwon River in 1837, Geelong was not incorporated as a town until 12 October 1849. The first council meeting was held, behind closed doors, on 9 February 1850 at the Royal Hotel, Malop Street.

Malop Street was always one of the principal streets. Here that great entrepreneur and actor, George Coppin, built a theatre. One of the shows, put on at one o'clock in the morning for the diggers of Ballarat enjoying a night out, included 'Railroad Station', a burlesque which coincided with the commencement of the Melbourne-Geelong railway.

At first the line didn't reach as far as Melbourne; it ended at Newport. The Governor, Sir Henry Barkly, opened the line in June 1857; he led a procession in which railway men carried picks and shovels and Aborigines bore in front of them free dinners donated by 'worthy citizens' and wore striped blankets and caps given by the government. On the train journey to Newport Henry Walters, the locomotive superintendent, was swept off the train as it was going under a low bridge. The train could not take all the additional guests invited on the return trip and top-hatted men not only had to miss their trip but had to help to push the train to get it started.

Today, Geelong has a port so effectively planned that it now handles more tonnage annually than all but four Australian ports. Many businessmen commute by rail between ever-spreading Geelong and Melbourne.

Malop Street, Geelong, looking East.

PALL MALL, SANDHURST

The mercantile activity of Sandhurst is concentrated on this spot, and towards evening the aspect of the place resembles that of a crowded London thoroughfare. The rise of Sandhurst, like that of most other towns upon the gold fields, has been extremely rapid, and the extent and richness of its quartz-reefs have combined to consolidate its prosperity. Elegant shops, spacious hotels, commodious theatres and concert rooms, and substantial dwelling houses, render it difficult to believe that the place is only ten years old, and that at the beginning of 1851, the soil, which is now honey-combed by the operations of the miner, was a mere sheep-walk, and its marvellous stores of treasure utterly unsuspected. When Mr Howitt visited Sandhurst in 1854, he witnessed, he says, the first introduction of machinery. At this present time (1861) there are not less than 144 steam engines employed in winding, pumping, puddling, crushing and other mining processes in this district, and the approximate value of the whole of the mining plant is £283,110. The number of miners engaged is 14,048, and the quantity of gold sent down by escort in 1860 was 346,603 ounces. Sandhurst supports two daily papers; two theatres are nightly open for the entertainment of the public.

From the beginning Pall Mall was not only an important thoroughfare in Sandhurst (Bendigo) but an elegant one. In 1857 'town allotments', as they were called, were in great demand and in the Mall prices were as high as £50 a foot; only six years before these allotments had been part of a large sheep run called Ravenswood, owned by Charles Sherrard. One explanation of the origin of the name 'Bendigo' is that Sherrard had a shepherd or hutkeeper who was a useful bruiser and had been named Bendigo after the celebrated English prizefighter. The part of Ravenswood which was his responsibility had a creek which was known as Bendigo's Creek, and when gold was found nearby the name was adopted. In 1890 a commission of enquiry investigating the discovery of gold in Bendigo reported that the area was known as Bendigo as far back as 1840 and that it got its name from an employee at Ravenswood. Other explanations of the name are that it is a corruption of 'Bandicoot', or that it came from an old Australian expression 'Around the bend I go'.

Later, the town was renamed Sandhurst by a local gold commissioner in honour of his father, who was a governor of Sandhurst Military College in England. But Bendigo was too good a name to lose, and in 1891 at a poll of citizens, the city was given back its first name.

Bendigo has had a long history of gold but, as early as 1855, many pessimists were prophesying that, with the gradual disappearance of the original alluvial gold, the town was doomed. About that time, however, Bendigo's gold king, George Lansell, was losing interest in making soap, candles and tallow and began to study quartz mining. Twice he lost heavily in deep-mining ventures but he continued to buy shares in one mining company after another. He saw a future in using steam power not only to speed up haulage and crushing operations, but to ventilate deep mines. By the mid-sixties his mines began to pay and he was soon known all over Australia as the 'Quartz King'. He left Australia in 1880 but seven years later he received in London a magnificently illuminated scroll signed by 2,628 Bendigo citizens imploring him to come back. He returned, was given a royal welcome and settled down with his family in his magnificent home Fortuna in Bendigo. When he died in 1906, he was reckoned to be worth £3,000,000.

Pall Mall, Sandhurst

Sands, Kenny & Co. Melbourne   Sands & Kenny Sydney

VIEW POINT, SANDHURST

Situated in the heart of an auriferous district and surrounded by some of the richest quartz reefs in Victoria, the prosperity of Sandhurst rests upon a durable basis, and the place itself is one of the most important inland towns. The rateable value of the real property within the limits of the municipality exceeds one million sterling. It possesses numerous manufactories, an energetic population, and its mineral resources are apparently inexhaustible; with such elements of success in its favour its progress in wealth and population has been very rapid, and is likely to be still more so when it shall have been brought into railway communication with the River Murray.

View Point did not get its name officially until 18 November 1959, although that name had been used for it from the earliest days, as part of Charing Cross, still regarded as the centre of Bendigo (Sandhurst). But for many years View Point was just as often called Jackson's Corner, after the store owned by a pioneer of the city, who was also a councillor, part-owner of a newspaper, mine manager and gold-mine speculator, not to mention a family man with eleven children.

Jackson attracted many customers to View Point with his store which sold groceries, ironmongery, general stores and drapery and also bought gold. Alongside his store was the Bank of New South Wales, and nearby were another gold buyer, an American stove depot, a tent maker, and a soap and candle factory run by a man yet to make his name in gold mining—George Lansell. On the opposite side of the street was the Bank of Victoria. By 1862, when this drawing was made, View Point was rapidly becoming the shopping centre of the town, and when the Melbourne to Bendigo railway was opened on 10 October great crowds of spectators were drawn to the 'magnificent display of gold nuggets in the Bank of New South Wales, the Bank of Victoria and Henry Jackson's splendid establishment'.

On the opening day, the Governor Sir Henry Barkly and his suite, with another five hundred official guests, arrived at 1 p.m., and by nightfall about twenty thousand merrymakers were enjoying the excitement, which included a monster dinner for eight hundred guests and a ball that lasted until dawn. Because the engine was unable to make the return journey the same night, many passengers who could not find lodgings, or even a made-up bed in a pew, joined the dancers. However, many ladies preferred to spend the night in first class carriages: 'here lay a lady with her delicate head on a gent's lap . . . here an elegant lady sobbed . . . . there a matronly one grieved . . . . or snored.' The finishing touch to an eventful night came when the train engine set fire to the huge triumphal arch over the line and destroyed it.

The days that followed were more efficiently organized. Trains ran three times daily each way, taking only four and a half hours for the hundred-mile journey. This, with return fares at 47s. 3d. and 34s. 9d., attracted many passengers who remembered arriving in Bendigo years before 'footsore, swag laden and weary at the end of a pilgrimage which only hope made endurable'. Among them was Henry Jackson who made View Point important.

View Point, Sandhurst.

Sands, Kenny & Co. Melbourne   Sands & Kenny, Sydney

TOWN AND MELBOURNE & HOBSON'S BAY RAILWAY PIERS, SANDRIDGE

A few years ago the whole of the sea-borne merchandise which entered the port of Melbourne was transhipped into lighters from vessels lying in the Bay, and was thence conveyed, by a slow and sinuous course, to the wharves on the banks of the Yarra, to which it is impracticable for ships of any magnitude to ascend. The cost, delay and, inconvenience of this proceeding led several projectors to prepare plans for a ship-canal to be cut from Sandridge to Melbourne, with docks and warehouses on either side; but the execution of such a scheme appears to be somewhat remote; and in the meantime the Melbourne and Hobson's Bay Railway Company have projected their pier into the Bay sufficiently far to enable vessels of the largest class to be alongside and discharge their cargoes into the railway trucks. As many as six or eight London and Liverpool liners may be seen simultaneously unloading at this pier, while the various steamers engaged in the intercolonial trade, resort to one or other of the two piers represented in the annexed picture, for the purposes of embarking and dis-embarking passengers and goods. Steamers ply regularly between Melbourne and Sydney, Adelaide, Launceston, Hobart Town, Port Albert (Gipps Land), Portland, Belfast, Warrnambool, Geelong and New Zealand; and it is not improbable that direct communication will be shortly opened up with Queensland, the youngest and most northerly of the Australian group of Colonies.

The opening of the Melbourne and Hobson's Bay railway between the city and Sandridge (Port Melbourne) was the first step towards making the port an effective one from which goods, passengers and general freight could be readily transported into the centre of the city. But it was the building of 'two great piers, erected at great expense' which revolutionised port traffic and railway operations. The shares of the railway company had been selling at a heavy discount. They quickly became a good investment when the line showed big profits and paid a 14 per cent dividend.

During the year 1859, more than half a million passengers used the three-mile railway line to Melbourne, the company's profit rose to £29,000 and over two thousand ships discharged cargo at the port. Some had thought that the railway pier, 1,746 feet long, was too exposed for safety in rough weather and many gloomily predicted that it would give a poor return for the £365,240 spent on it. But the pessimists were soon shown that the largest ships could berth alongside both piers; cargo was loaded direct into railway trucks at the station pier, and on to lorries and drays at the town pier. The building of a duplicate line in 1858 and of a second railway bridge over the Yarra speeded up traffic. In the same year the station pier was lengthened to 1,871 feet and widened to sixty feet. Trains ran every half hour and steamers between Sandridge and Williamstown sailed every hour. All this helped to make the pier one of the most popular promenades on Sunday afternoon. 'It was a sight,' says one writer, 'to see the brass buttoned apprentices, always spoken of as middies, who had come from the sailing ships lying alongside, walking slowly and looking out for company.'

With the coming of the railway, the fleet of coaches that ran between the beach and the city disappeared. But the coach drivers must have enjoyed the moment on the opening day of the railway when the locomotive refused to start on its homeward journey and the Governor, Sir Charles Hotham, an old naval commander, 'strode up and down the platform using it like a quarterdeck, scowling and stern, as though to quell a mutiny'. The little train started on its way only with the help of twenty burly policemen, weighing an average of fourteen stone, who 'literally put their shoulders to the wheel'.

Town, and Melbourne & Hobson's Bay Railway Piers, Sandridge.

Sands Kenny & C° Melbourne _ Sands & Kenny, Sydney.

JOHNSTON STREET BRIDGE, OVER THE YARRA, STUDLEY PARK

122 One of the most picturesque spots in the vicinity of Melbourne lies in immediate proximity to this bridge. The river winds round a lofty knoll, the declivitous sides of which are somewhat thickly timbered, and on the banks of the stream some magnificent willows, offshoots of the historical tree at St Helena, almost intercept, by their rich foliage the sunshine from the dark waters which flow beneath. On the western side of the river, vineyards and gardens in a high state of cultivation, slope down to the water's edge; while on the opposite bank, a Government reserve, designated Studley Park, retains most of the characteristics of the primitive bush. The fondness for old-world names displayed by colonists is shown in the choice of the appellations bestowed upon neighbouring localities. 'Abbotsford' and 'Saint Heliers' perpetuate recollections of the banks of the Tweed and the island of Jersey; and the villages of Kew, Eltham, Northcote and Heidelberg owe their titles to an equally remote and obvious source. As a general rule the native names are far preferable, more euphonious, and entitled to preservation as indicating, in most instances, some physical peculiarity of the place or district. Booroondara, the aboriginal designation of a parish adjoining Kew, is a good specimen of the musical epithets employed by the blacks for the purpose of distinguishing certain localities, and offers a remarkable contrast to the capriciously selected names conferred by miners upon places in the interior, such for example as Dead Horse Gully, Murderer's Flat, Lucky Woman's, Pickpocket, Peg-leg Gully, Lob's Hole and the like.

This is one of the loveliest reaches of the Yarra. It is still possible to hire a rowboat at Studley Park and enjoy a quiet journey along the willow-covered banks down to Dight's Falls overlooked by the 'lofty knoll' mentioned in the original caption which is now topped by a memorial cairn recalling the first overlanders. From across the Murray River, John Gardiner, Joseph Hawdon and Captain Hepburn, who drove their cattle across the Yarra near this point.

The original Johnston Street Bridge, erected in 1857, was badly tilted by a great flood during which the river rose 36 feet, and it was not replaced until 1876. It is still there, but a smaller bridge that was built nearby and named the Studley Park Bridge has long since disappeared. This was always called the 'Penny' bridge, not only because that was the price of the toll for pedestrians, but because it was kept by Thomas Halfpenny.

Today this stretch of river looks much the same as it does in the engraving—except that the vineyards have disappeared. These produced much good wine but did not last as long as those further up the river near Yarra Glen. At the International Exhibition in 1881 in Melbourne, with entries from all parts of the world, a trophy donated by the Emperor of Germany was awarded to the wine from St Huberts, part of the estate of Yering which at that time was producing 70,000 gallons of wine a year.

Now that more Victorians are drinking wine, the names of courageous viticulturalists like William Ryrie, who established the first Yarra vineyard in 1837, Paul de Castella and Andrew Rowan should not be forgotten.

Johnston Street Bridge, over the Yarra, Studley Park.

Sands, Kenny & Co Melbourne. Sands & Kenny, Sydney.

MELBOURNE, ST. KILDA & BRIGHTON RAILWAY BRIDGE, ST. KILDA ROAD

The accompanying engraving represents a portion of the line of railway which connects Melbourne with a chain of suburbs stretching eastward along the northern shore of Hobson's Bay. Ultimately, as population increases and settlement extends, this line will be prolonged, in all probability, until it reaches the coal fields in the district of Western Port, at present it is used for passenger traffic exclusively.

This bridge carried the St Kilda–Windsor loop line across St Kilda Road. The line, owned by the new St Kilda and Brighton Railway Company, had been opened on 3 December 1859 when the directors and a few friends and parliamentarians had boarded a two-carriage train at midday. The journey through St Kilda and Windsor ended at Bay Street, Brighton, where the party was met by cheering navvies who had obviously celebrated the occasion. Two three-horse omnibuses then took them on to the Brighton Hotel where they enjoyed a 'sumptuous repast'. On their return to the station, they were so flattered by the repeated cheers of the navvies that they arranged a series of impromptu foot races and gave a prize of a purse of money.

Ten days later the loop line was opened to the public but people never really took to it. When the St Kilda and Brighton Railway Company was taken over by the Melbourne and Suburban Railway, the line was shut down—on 20 September 1862. The venture had cost something like £70,000.

The abutments of the St Kilda Road bridge and the wing walls were of bluestone, while the side piers were solid bluegum poles in pairs. The 42-foot central arch was 15 feet above the ground at its highest level, while the two side arches were footways 20 feet wide.

The loop line was an interesting piece of local engineering. It ran first in a north-easterly direction from St Kilda railway station, along an embankment 15 feet high and 700 feet long which skirted the southern end of Albert Park lake. The embankment was followed by an equally long wooden viaduct spanning a large swamp that spilled away from the lake. This viaduct was supported by bluegum piers driven 15 feet into the soggy ground. At each end of the viaduct was a carriageway spanned by a central arch with two side ones for pedestrians. Beyond the viaduct the line was carried by an earthen embankment again until it reached St Kilda Road and later Punt Road, both spanned by bridges. The line was well-planned even to the making of the embankments with the earth from the Windsor railway cutting; it also followed the excellent principle of doing without level crossings.

In March 1869 the Prahran councillors showed by direct action what they thought about level crossings. Exasperated by expensive delays at the Union Street level crossing in their municipality, they met there on a cold morning just before dawn with their Town Clerk, borough solicitor and a gang of workmen. As first light came, the shivering workers raced out with 'crowbars, picks and shovels to tear up the line'. No attempt was made to disguise the noise—even had that been possible—and the area was soon filled with enthusiastic locals. Indignant railway officials, accompanied by the police, also arrived and for a few minutes battle seemed likely. But the bystanders were disappointed. The argument was finally settled in a court which decided that the railway owners had the right to continue using the crossing.

Melbourne, St. Kilda & Brighton Railway Bridge, St. Kilda Road.

Sands, Kenny & Co. Melbourne _ Sands & Kenny, Sydney.

BALLAARAT EAST FROM THE CAMP RESERVE, MOUNT BUNINYONG IN THE DISTANCE

The whole of the valley intervening between the slight eminence from which this view is taken and Mount Buninyong, visible in the distance, is one vast depository of gold, so capriciously distributed that while masses have been exhumed sufficiently heavy to task a strong man to lift them, some of the soil washed was only just sufficiently impregnated with the precious metal to remunerate the patient and easily contented Chinaman. Originally celebrated for the richness of its surface diggings, Ballarat has now gained a celebrity of another kind. Deep sinkings, effected by associated effort, and the co-operation of labour, capital and machinery, have revealed the existence of gutters of gold lying at the depth of 400 and 500 feet below the surface; while the quartz reefs of the district, though poor in quality, are comparatively inexhaustible, and yield a handsome return to the various companies engaged in working them.

Ballarat East, containing a population of 13,000 inhabitants, consists chiefly of one long street, known as the Main Road, lined with shops and taverns lighted with gas, which presents, on a Saturday evening, a scene as animated as any to be met with in the most thronged thoroughfares of London. In one portion of the Main Road there is a cluster of stores and restaurants occupied by Chinamen, and in another part of the town the same people have formed a populous encampment and erected a commodious Joss-House. About 2,500 Chinamen are engaged in mining operations on Ballarat, while the number of Europeans occupied in those pursuits is about 10,000, and the approximate value of the steam engines and machinery they employ (most of which is now manufactured on the spot) is £320,000. The aggregate yield of this gold-field during the year 1860 was 267,228 ounces, of the value in round numbers of one million sterling.

The Camp Reserve at Ballarat was on the site of that part of Camp Street between Sturt and Mair Streets where the Public Library and Police Headquarters were built. Originally the police and military camp stood here.

It was certainly no exaggeration to claim, as the original caption does, that some nuggets needed strong arms to lift them and it was pardonable exaggeration to say that the area was one vast depository of gold. For the view away to Mount Buninyong lay across the famous Canadian gully. Here, as early as February 1853 three miners—Bristow, Sully and Gough—who had been about to give up mining in disgust, discovered the 'Canadian' nugget, weighing 1,017 ounces. A few days later they brought up the 'Wonder' nugget which weighed 1,011 ounces. In the same week, Evans and Green, in the claim next to these three lucky diggers, unearthed the 'Sarah Sands' nugget; 101 pounds of almost solid gold. Two other miners, Joyce and Welsh, in the next week and within forty feet of the original discoveries, were more than happy with their smaller nuggets of 368 and 371 ounces. Not far from this concentration of gold the lovely 'Lady Hotham' of 1,117 ounces was found, as well as a nest of smaller nuggets weighing 165 pounds!

Only a few chains away from Canadian Gully, the rewards in Prince Regent Gully were so rich that it was called 'the jeweller's shop'. At times the pay dirt brought up from shafts contained almost as much gold as clay, and yielded between £1,300 and £2,000 a foot. In one session of 54 hours, Gardiner's party washed out 3,040 ounces worth £12,000. A party of men nearby—guarding their find and afraid to move from the mine—won £8,000 in a week. The fantastic Blacksmith's Hole was also nearby—a claim only 24 feet square which produced for its fortunate owners one ton of gold worth £142,000, or about $1,000,000 today. The Canadian Gully deep quartz mines were also very rich—both the North Woah Hawp (1,375 feet) and New Normanby (1,590 feet) yielded gold worth more than $2,000,000 in today's money.

Ballaarat East from the Camp Reserve, Mount Buninyong in the Distance.

Sands Kenny & Co. Melbourne.   Sands & Kenny, Sydney.

POST & TELEGRAPH OFFICES & MECHANICS' INSTITUTE, CASTLEMAINE

Castlemaine ranks third in point of productiveness among the Victorian gold-fields, the escort returns from this district, in the year 1860, amounting to 223,690 ounces. The town lies in the midst of picturesque scenery, and has been laid out with a more judicious regard to present convenience and future extension than is usually exhibited in determining the sites and defining the plans of colonial townships. Its spacious Market Square is surrounded by substantial buildings; and while private enterprise is steadily improving the place, the subsidies or grants-in-aid annually voted by the Legislature, have been applied to the embellishment of Castlemaine by the erection of edifices like those represented in the accompanying plate. When the Census of 1857 was taken, the population of the Warden's district of Castlemaine was found to consist of 31,331 persons occupying 10,222 houses; 23,808 persons living in tents or 'camping out', and 4,668 Chinese. The Census for 1861 will necessarily show a large increase on these numbers, while a great alteration will have taken place in the nature of the abodes occupied, owing to the substitution of more settled habits for the nomadic tendencies which formerly characterised our mining population, and the extension of tillage in the vicinity of the principal gold-fields. In some instances the pursuit of quartz mining is combined with that of agriculture; and the operations on the 'reef' are suspended while the harvest is being gathered in; after which they are resumed, until the period for sowing the crops arrives, and reclaims the attention of the farming 'reefer'.

The 1861 census for Castlemaine mentioned in the original caption showed no increase, although the number of Chinese had risen to more than 7,500, a third of the population. Nor was the quartz mining profitable. Its yield was poor compared with that in Ballarat and Bendigo and attempts were made to reduce costs by using water instead of steam power. The biggest water-wheel erected in the district—built by the Madame Garfield Company—had a diameter of sixty six feet. But these and other large wheels were not the solution, and the returns stayed depressingly low.

If Castlemaine did not expand as much as was hoped in those days, it has the consolation of having been able to keep many historic buildings. Several good examples are shown in this engraving. First on the right is the courthouse which was erected in 1860. Next is the police court and post office which was replaced by the present building in 1875. The Roman Catholic Church behind the post office is still used. The telegraphic office was erected in 1857; its centre block and right wing are now used as the headquarters of the Castlemaine Old Pioneers' Association. The building on the extreme left is the Mechanics' Institute built in the same year; although greatly changed in appearance by additions, it is still used as the Castlemaine Library and Library Hall.

It was here, in 1857, that one of the most famous Castlemaine breakfasts was given by one hundred prominent citizens to the Governor, Sir Henry Barkly. The charge was one and a half guineas but this appears reasonable for the mouth-watering menu on which the entrees alone numbered fourteen, ranging from eels en turban, iced ham and snipe en Belle-vue, to 'Patties à la Espagnole.'

Castlemaine offers the visitor the experience of looking at old prints and paintings at the local gallery or museum and, then going out into the town and looking at the originals.

Post & Telegraph Offices & Mechanics Institute, Castlemaine.

Sands Kenny & Co Melbourne. Sands & Kenny Sydney.